C000000911

HOPE FOR TH

Alan Brunskill Webster's life and career brought him into contact with thousands of people from all walks of life. His response to this was to understand and reflect on the lives of all those his ministry touched – believers, half-believers and doubters, and country people and city magnates.

He served in parishes in Sheffield and Barnard Castle, and was on the staff of Westcott House, Cambridge and Warden of Lincoln Theological College, when he also served as a Canon of Lincoln Cathedral. During the 1970s and 1980s, he was Dean of Norwich and then of St Paul's Cathedral in London. He was honoured with the KCVO and with an honorary DD from the City University, London. He died in September 2007.

HOPE FOR THE FUTURE

People who made a difference

Alan Webster

First published in Great Britain in 2008

Society for Promoting Christian Knowledge
36 Causton Street
London SW1P 4ST

British Library Cataloguing-in-Publication Data
A catalogue record for this book is available from the British Library

ISBN 978–0–281–06000–9

1 3 5 7 9 10 8 6 4 2

Typeset by Graphicraft Ltd, Hong Kong
Printed in Great Britain by Ashford Colour Press

Produced on paper from sustainable forests

For Margaret

CONTENTS

Editors' Note   xi
Foreword by Owen Chadwick   xiii

Theme 1: Leaders and the Church   1

Mikhail Gorbachev   1
A tale of two archbishops   3
Robert Runcie   6
Geoffrey Fisher   7
Leslie Hunter   9
David Sheppard   12
Poul Hartling   15
Leslie Brown   16

Theme 2: World Peace, Justice and Tolerance   19

Politicians as peacemakers   19
Religion and honesty   21
John Taylor   23
Norwich and the Ugandan Asians   25
Prayer versus dogma   27
Gonville ffrench-Beytagh   29
A fusion of the spiritual and the secular   32
Working together   34
More than conquerors   36

Theme 3: Opening Up the Church   43

Julian of Norwich   43
Florence Tim Oi Li   45
Christian Howard   47
Sister Hilary of Wantage   49
Building bridges from the City   53
Constructive disagreement   55
Can cathedrals share the sorrows and joys of
    their cities?   57

The Church's one foundation 59
Alan Ecclestone 61
Edward Carpenter 64
Kenneth Sansbury 67
Oliver Tomkins 70
Horace Dammers 73
Jim Bishop 75
Stanley Booth-Clibborn 77

Theme 4: The Church in Action **81**
Cure of souls 81
Launcelot Fleming 82
Kenneth Riches 85
Edward Patey 87
Francis House 90
Frank Wright 92
John Tinsley 94
Joan Ramsey 97
Village churches 98

Theme 5: Enriching Human Life **101**
All shall be well 101
A stay in hospital is a lesson in the meaning and
    value of trust 103
Rogues of profit still haunt the celestial road 105
Threefold cord of religion, science and literature in
    the character of Sir Thomas Browne 107
Petra Clarke 113
Humanity should relish the precious mysteriousness
    of life 114
Charles Groves 116
Tom Baker 119

Theme 6: Children and Young People **123**
God backs the poor 123
Choice for changing faith 126
Why the kids are all right 128
High ideals for the next generation 130

Contents

Epilogue: Hope for the Future   **133**

   The journey towards understanding   133

   Everyday resurrections   135

   Love is at the heart of human life   137

The Very Revd Alan Webster   **139**

Sources and Acknowledgements   **143**

EDITORS' NOTE

Working together with Alan Webster, we have chosen a selection from two groups of Alan's writings over the previous decades. Some of these are articles with a wide-ranging topic, many of them contributions to the 'Credo' series printed in *The Times*, which discuss the work of the Church in the world today. Others are his appreciative tributes to individual people he has known, who have spent their lives in the service of the Church and of others. In the process of selection, a series of themes emerged, so that each of the articles offers accounts of people whose gifts lay in a particular aspect of the Church's work: pastoral care, world justice and peace, and many more.

Since many of these personal tributes originally appeared as obituaries, one focus of the book is on past achievements. But this book is not just a celebration of the past; it looks at the present and towards the future with equal conviction and hope. In our work as volunteers at Norwich Cathedral, we are constantly aware of the vast range of people who come there, looking for, and often finding, something deeper than the merely mundane and secular. Alan's articles demonstrate ways in which the Church is aware of their needs, sometimes more aware than they themselves are, and is working to respond to them.

'As a sense of religion declines, we feel the want of it in every branch of social life.' So wrote the Revd George Burton from Thetford in Norfolk to a friend and fellow-clergyman in London, equally concerned about the decay of Christian belief and practice. Burton expressed concern over the growth of 'superstition and fanaticism . . . folly and atheism'. This seems a modern sentiment, but the year is 1758, a time which supporters and opponents of the Church alike tend to look back to these days as still an 'age of faith'. Our modern media are full of claims that the Church, and the Christianity that drives it, is not just declining today but is in its last stages in Britain, a decrepit creature creeping towards extinction as society grows ever more secular. Yet a look into the past, even earlier than Burton's days, will show similar fears and concerns.

But this negative view, whether the wish-fulfilment of secularists or the secret fear of churchgoers, is far from the whole story: indeed, the reverse could be argued to be the case. The enjoyable process of working with Alan Webster to select the contents for this book has reinforced our understanding that the Spirit is as active in the Church and the world today as it has ever been. It is the same world, and the same Spirit, doing amazing things in all kinds of ways to answer the needs of that world and its people.

This is not just a book about 'faith' in the sense that the modern media use the word, to mean strict adherence to a set of beliefs, but about the implications of faith – putting belief into daily action for the good of others. Activity is one of the keynotes of this book; a subtitle for it could perhaps be 'Belief in Action'. Alan Webster has drawn on the experience of a long and varied lifetime to bring together the lives of a group of remarkable people, all of whom acted as they did because of their firm Christian belief, and who knew that this belief required positive action.

So in response to George Burton's concern, we offer Archbishop John Sentamu's claim to the General Synod in the summer of 2007. Urging the Church to throw off fear of failure and inadequacy, he challenged them, and us, to look at what is really happening in the Church's work in the world: 'We are doing big stuff!'

Alan Webster's book shows how the people of the Church, past and present, have been guided by the Spirit to do 'big stuff', and points the way to even greater stuff tomorrow.

Diana and Michael Honeybone

FOREWORD

Alan Webster was master of an art where masters are rare and which only existed from about the time of the Napoleonic Wars. He wrote excellent obituaries and was often invited to contribute such notices of persons who had just died. The idea of this book came when friends pleaded that these types of short article should be collected and printed; for they could help not only history but religion.

His character was of the gentlest. Everyone enjoyed talking to him. He had two vocations which were far apart. He trained future priests, who were largely middle class because of the need that they should have higher education. But he thought most about human beings on the margins of society: unemployed, ill-paid, waterless, housed in filthiness; Africans in an apartheid regime; Latin Americans who needed liberation. These concerns made him a man of the Left. He approved of bishops who walked in protest processions against the closing of factories, whereby many were made unemployed. Probably the bishop he most admired was Leslie Hunter of Sheffield, who used to meet trade union leaders by night. He kept in mind victims of police tyranny such as Steve Biko or Oscar Romero; he liked the possibility that Marxists and Christians could agree in their quest to make society less unequal. Nowhere near a Communist himself, he admired rare Anglican clergymen who were Communists. In his eyes, it was a virtue that we should be angry with society as it is. He had no desire that clergy should refrain from politics. He admired a bishop who said that the idea that religion does not mix with politics is a very English way of sitting on the fence. He preferred bishops in the House of Lords to take the Labour whip. He was far too peaceable a person to lead a militant campaign. He found Canon Collins, who led such campaigns effectively, difficult as a colleague.

Webster had always been strong for the ordination of women to the priesthood, partly on grounds of pastoral need but more from a conviction that human beings were being ill-treated by an establishment; in this case, the victims were women. He was afraid that sinister conservative forces worked to keep the best men and women down or the best policies frustrated because they would force change.

This attractive, humane, civilized man had to bear abuse. A politician called him a wimp. When he was Dean of Norwich and ensured a welcome in Norfolk for refugees from the Ugandan tyrant Amin, some critics hoped that he would house them all in the Norwich deanery.

He loved his Church. Yet he did not love what he called narrow ecclesiastical attitudes. A Church too, with its strong sense of history, can block change. He was charitable to people who opposed him. In some ways, Archbishop Fisher of Canterbury was Webster's ecclesiastical opposite: a dominant chairman, a worker for order in the Church, a financier who understood that money counts even in churches, a disciplinarian who demanded that everyone keep the rules. Webster could write gratefully about his achievement. And yet he believed that, under Fisher, the Church turned inward upon itself, devoting so many hours to its constitution, its law, its way of worship; and, for Webster, the Church mattered only if it was moving away from itself and outward towards human beings – whether they were church members or not, whether they were Christians or not. Fisher wanted everything to be tidy. Webster did not mind if the Church was tidy but it could not be very tidy if it moved out towards the downtrodden.

The shrines of churches should not be bland. He had a nagging sense that things were wrong if the Church was comfortable. It must listen; and if it really listened it must hear the sighs of sufferers from across the world. If we try to change things, we meet a cross. That makes it impossible to be too comfortable.

Deans of cathedrals are respected as eminent in an establishment and as persons who care for the most important acts of worship in the kingdom. Webster was successively dean of two of the most celebrated and visited places of prayer. He had to engage with order and ceremony and music, and, at times, with what is grand. Yet somehow his gentle personality and affection for the people around him made the praise and the quiet inner centre dominate the outward show. Webster liked a happy vagueness in ceremonial processions. He expressed his ideal for a service thus: brevity, time for silence, reflection and meditation.

He cared more for the immediacy of God than for descriptions or doctrines about God. The writers about religion whom he admired were those who had a half-inarticulate vision of a reality which is divine, such as von Hügel and John Taylor. He had the contemplative side which loved the peace of thinking about truth in the beauty and solitude of a garden. He had a feeling that poetry could come nearer to God than prose. Experience was more important to him than words.

A person whom he admired among the saints was Julian of Norwich. Webster was determined that Christians should go out and be active in the world, yet Julian was a hermit who retreated and left the world to get on as best it could. However, she confronted God in her sanctuary and was full of joy.

Owen Chadwick

Theme I

LEADERS AND THE CHURCH

This book brings together the lives of some remarkable people, their hopes for the world and the work they did to fulfil these hopes. This first chapter strikes one of the keynotes of the book. It considers people who gave leadership and encouragement when these were most needed. Like the other people in this collection, they offer inspiration to those facing new challenges today.

Mikhail Gorbachev

Mikhail Gorbachev wrote to *The Times* in March to remind us of his and President Reagan's statement in 1985 that 'a nuclear war cannot be won and must never be fought'. It was also a reminder of the good fortune of his partially Christian upbringing – no doubt this was one of the reasons that, with Margaret Thatcher, he and President Reagan kept the peace.

He described the secular and the spiritual in his childhood home as 'peaceful coexistence'. He lived in the Caucasus during the Second World War, in which his father fought, as his grandfather had fought in the First. The family room had on one side a bookshelf with booklets by Marx, Engels and Lenin. The other corner had an icon and an icon lamp and underneath, on a homemade table, stood the portraits of Lenin and Stalin. Gorbachev's grandmother was deeply religious but his grandfather was not a believer. Neither his grandparents nor his parents were troubled by this clash of faiths, and both were respected. They left it to the young Mikhail, later a

1

student at Moscow University where he met his wife Raisa, who was reading philosophy, to work out the coexistence on the national arena.

Gorbachev visited London twice, first in 1981 as Secretary of the Communist Party and five years later with Raisa as ruler of the Soviet Union. On his first visit the authorities had arranged that he should see the Tower of London but on the day itself he decided instead to stop his motorcade at St Paul's and he came unannounced to be received by the vergers. He was as inquisitive as he was with world rulers and enquired what the dome was for. The dean's verger gave a firmly uncompromising reply: 'Sir, in order to worship God.'

When he visited St Paul's more formally years later with Raisa and their daughter, preparations for Christmas were going on in the cathedral. The visitors were fascinated by the crib carved by Astrid Zidower, the Polish artist, who emphasized the struggle needed to get to Bethlehem, with its figures outside the stable peering through cracks in its walls.

When Mrs Thatcher visited Russia, arrangements were made for her to light a candle at the monastery at Zagorsk. In the era of perestroika space was found for the spirit even in an officially atheist country.

Converting what Marxism would call 'the Christian myth' into reality is giving active love real power in social, economic and political life. In his last address to Soviet citizens as President of the Soviet Union, on 25 December 1991, Gorbachev said: 'We live in a new world. An end has been put to the Cold War, the arms race and the insane militarization of our country, which crippled our economy, distorted our thinking and undermined our morals.'

He saw that no one wanted to let go of power and so often used a bloody military short-cut to solve political problems that needed a patient, thoughtful approach.

Speaking to the students at the Sorbonne in 1989 he had insisted that politics, science and ethics should always be held together or the consequences would be fatal. He was working out, against an Enlightenment background, those childhood intuitions of the co-existence of Marx and the icon lamp. He also visited Pope John Paul II and established relations with the Vatican. Years before he had said to the British Parliament that 'Europe is our common home'.

He saw the Enlightenment and the Spirit as both part of the human inheritance.

The world needs moments when those with strong but differing convictions can work together for the common good. The World Health Organization, which spearheads the fight against the Aids pandemic, has staff members with strong religious convictions and with none.

Dr Petra Clarke, who led the London delegates in the General Synod vote to ordain women, worked for women raped in Bulawayo and became a doctor in the Medical Foundation for the Care of Victims of Torture – trying to heal very different victims with different allies.

Amnesty International, Barnardo's and the Telephone Samaritans all depend on volunteers with various convictions.

In a talk for Lent Cherie Blair pointed out how those in England concerned with the rule of law and victim–oppressor reconciliation can learn from Zacchaeus (Luke 19.1–10), who met and repaid his victims.

Those symbols long ago in the Urals, where Gorbachev grew up, which spoke so effectively of 'peaceful coexistence', have never been more needed in our global society.

A tale of two archbishops

Two of the most distinguished archbishops of the twentieth century, Robert Runcie of Canterbury and Oscar Romero of El Salvador, experienced the crisis of their lives in the first few months of 1980. Both were seen by their contemporaries as heroes. London posters hailed Runcie as 'War Hero as Archbishop', since he had rescued a comrade from under a burning tank and received the Military Cross. Oscar Romero, in the course of the savage civil war in Central America, made 'a special plea to the men of the army . . . to stop the repression'. When celebrating Mass on Monday, 24 March 1980 in the Divina Providentia Hospital Chapel in San Salvador, a single shot rang out from a hired assassin as he said the words: 'Let us join together, then, . . . in faith and hope in this moment of prayer'. He was a true martyr.

Both had been chosen by their churches as archbishops because they were considered safe men who would not rock the ecclesiastical boat when radical reforms were being suggested. Oscar Romero was appointed in place of more aggressive candidates after serving as bishop of the diocese of Santiago de Maria (1974–7) and a period of study at Louvain University, where he enjoyed meeting reformers who were facing the secularization of Europe and took seriously the absence of faith among so many who are marginalized. They hoped the Church would liberate the poor. Romero said later, 'There is a way to know if God is near us or far away. Everyone who is concerned about the hungry, or the naked, or the poor, about the disappeared, about the tortured, about the prisoner, will find that God is near.' Central and South American bishops meeting at Medellín had reached similar conclusions.

In the civil war in El Salvador it is reckoned that 70,000 were killed, and the Church suffered with the people. When the young Jesuit priest, Fr Rutilio Grande, was assassinated by government forces alongside an old man and a boy on 12 March 1977, Romero cancelled all the Masses in the country but one Mass at the funeral. As the liberation theologian Fr Jon Sobrino SJ put it, 'I believe that the murder of Rutilio Grande was the occasion of the conversion of Archbishop Romero.' It was acts of such courage which led to Romero being sanctified by the people of El Salvador, though conservative forces in Europe forbid his official 'canonization'. To quote his own words:

> A prophet has to be angry with society, when society is not in accord with God. I base what I preach on Jesus. In Jesus is the truth of what I am saying. The Church today does not rely on any power, or wealth. Today the church is poor . . . Human beings are more children of God when they become more brotherly or sisterly to other human beings . . . the shepherd must be where the suffering is.

A few hours after the government's assassin's bullet killed Romero, Archbishop Robert Runcie was enthroned in Canterbury Cathedral. He was the first archbishop to be chosen by the newly created Crown Appointments Commission, provided by the former Labour Prime Minister Jim Callaghan to give weight to the Church's views. (On the Commission we noticed that the 10 Downing Street patronage secretary was present throughout and the more radical candidates in favour of the ordination of women and reunion with the free churches were at a disadvantage.) However, the service at Canterbury Cathedral was a splendid moment of national unity, with royalty, the government, the various churches and the political parties there to back the spiritual leadership which it was hoped Robert Runcie would give the nation. The special train from London to Canterbury and back to carry the congregation seemed to symbolize the friendliness of community so distant in those war-torn countries in Central America.

It was noticeable in England that as the years went by Archbishop Runcie became less conservative in politics, and his report *Faith in the City* was one of the causes of the change in economic policy registered at the 1997 election – a change which Mrs Thatcher herself had begun before the new interventionist policy of the Blair Labour government. After retirement Archbishop Runcie experienced a Eucharist in the United States that was celebrated by a woman, which liberated him from his earlier hesitations. When in 1986 an ecumenical group from London travelled to Central America to assist the peace movement in El Salvador, Guatemala and Nicaragua, his message to Romero's successor, presented at Mass close to Romero's tomb, revealed the depth of prayerful agreement between those two brave men faced with such different social problems. Like Archbishop Romero, Archbishop Runcie welcomed the slow changes in English social outlook – the opposition to apartheid, the quiet tolerance of minorities, homosexuals and the divorced, and a positive welcome to Christian socialists and liberal reformers, and the presence of women in all areas of leadership.

If you visit Archbishop Romero's grave in San Salvador Cathedral or Archbishop Runcie's at St Albans, you will no doubt feel that the Spirit used two brave men, both blessed with a sense of humour and prophecy, to serve the very different communities around them. It is liberating for the Church to evoke such leadership decade after decade.

Robert Runcie

The Falklands service

Runcie was neither a pacifist nor a jingoist, and always supported the British government's right to defend the Falkland Islands and the islanders from the Argentine invasion. But he was determined after the war, with the other church leaders, to emphasize the Pope's message, delivered at Coventry, that war is evil. Runcie's sermon at St Paul's, much attacked by the right wing, urged reconciliation and shared mourning by both British and Argentinian families who had lost relatives: 'A shared anguish can be a bridge of reconciliation. Our neighbours are indeed like us.' Many felt that he deserved a bar to his Military Cross for this sermon.[1] Margaret Thatcher, the prime minister, was critical and was restrained from taking the matter up in the House of Commons only by the personal intervention of the Duke of Edinburgh.

Faith in the City

This wounding campaign did not dampen Runcie's commitment to remain archbishop. He ignored those who demanded his resignation in favour of a hardline, illiberal and authoritarian archbishop. Instead he showed great skill and energy in facing the real needs of the inner cities, as riots disclosed the suffering of the unemployed and the dangers of poor schools and neglected housing in semi-derelict estates. The prime minister and her party appeared to think that 'There is no such thing as society' and to be abdicating responsibility. Church people and family members living in the inner cities and housing estates knew that England was in crisis.

Urged on by the urban bishops, especially David Sheppard of Liverpool and Jim Thompson of Stepney, with Canon Eric James as catalyst and Sir Richard O'Brien as determined but diplomatic chairman, Archbishop Runcie's report, *Faith in the City* (1985), became a banner for those with a sense of duty to society. It was initially denounced by a government minister as 'Marxist' but led to the church raising over £20 million for its urban fund. Runcie's speech in the Bank of England on 27 January 1987, at a meeting organized by St Paul's Cathedral and chaired by the governor, to involve the financial City, was passionate and powerful. The report came to be seen as a manifesto for the change in national policy which the 1997 general election finally effected. Some had realized that Runcie was the surrogate leader of the opposition. Diehards, such as Alan Clark MP, described him as a 'wimp'.

Lambeth Conference

The Lambeth Conference of 1988 was a triumph for Runcie's leadership, which had included so many visits to overseas churches. He took great trouble to get it well prepared and organized (in contrast to the 1978 and 1998 conferences). He held together the different views over the ordination of women and prevented the Anglican Communion from dividing into opposing factions. He was seen at his best as a wise, eirenic, witty and humane leader, pleading against isolated or alienating decisions. In South Africa, by early action on the Crown Appointments Commission, he had cleared the way by bringing home an English bishop, so that Archbishop Desmond Tutu could be appointed to give inspired leadership at Cape Town.

Note

1 For the full text, see Robert Runcie, *Windows Onto God* (London: SPCK, 1983); an account of the service itself is in Alan Webster, *Reaching for Reality* (London: SPCK, 2002).

Geoffrey Fisher

Archbishop Geoffrey Fisher's work for the worldwide Anglican Communion was outstanding. The growing importance of the ten-yearly Lambeth Conference as one of the world's most comprehensive Christian gatherings owes much to his vision and exertions. He travelled, often with Mrs Fisher, to all parts of the Commonwealth and beyond. He wrote innumerable letters to overseas bishops, clergy, and lay people and gave thought to and ingenious suggestions for creating an infrastructure which could hold the Communion together during the ten-year intervals between the conferences. Unlike the Vatican he encouraged autonomy and was prepared to trust to provincial good sense to balance diocesan eccentricity and even in some cases tribalism. There are now, thanks largely to Fisher, a large majority of non-English bishops among the nearly 800 bishops attending the Lambeth Conferences. He did not succeed in endowing all the provinces he created and left his successors an almost impossibly heavy burden requiring exceptional resources of intelligent diplomacy.

Fisher was one of the presidents of the World Council of Churches (1946–54). Between 1946 and 1960 he visited the United States and Canada several times and in 1950 New Zealand and Australia, where the creation of provinces was complex and controversial thanks to the evangelical individuality of the Diocese of Sydney. He visited West Africa in 1951, Central Africa in 1955, Nigeria and East Africa in 1960. Only in Central Africa did he become embroiled in political controversy over the proposed federation and made a resented remark about all men enjoying equality in the love of God but not in the sight of God. In 1959 he visited India, Japan and Korea and again found constitution-making congenial. He was always willing to divest Canterbury of direct responsibility. He gave additional duties to the archbishopric of Jerusalem. Occasionally he intervened. Like many others in London he found it hard to take a tough line on behalf of a few brave South African Anglicans in their determined and dangerous struggles with the apartheid government. Fisher rebuked Trevor Huddleston for his campaign and agreed with the Community of the Resurrection when it recalled him. He regretted efforts to bring the ordination of women before the 1948 Lambeth Conference. Eventually this became a major issue in 1988 and was accepted for England by the General Synod in 1992. Fisher had not rejected the possibility outright, but coming from the old tradition of single-sex schools and universities he did not foresee that the bar against women's ordination would soon appear an injustice.

Of all Fisher's journeys his visit to Jerusalem, Istanbul and Rome at the end of 1960 was the most memorable. No Archbishop of Canterbury had talked with the Pope since 1397. Geoffrey Fisher and John XXIII got on well: 'We talked as two happy people who had seen a good deal of the world, and of life, and of the churches' was how Fisher described his meeting afterwards.[1] In speaking to the Pope, he said: 'We are each now running on parallel courses; we are looking forward, until, in God's good time, our two courses approximate and meet.' After a momentary hesitation the Pope replied: 'You are right.'[2] Pope John said to an Anglican visitor the following year: 'There is a straightforward man, of high ideals and great sincerity. I see many people here from kings to the least of men; but I knew at once that he was a man of God.'[3] This conversation opened a new era in Roman Catholic–Anglican relations which was further encouraged by the Vatican Council and despite many setbacks has continued, especially among the lay people of the two churches throughout the world.

Notes

1 Edward Carpenter, *Archbishop Fisher: His Life and Times* (Norwich: Canterbury Press, 1991), p. 737.
2 *The Dictionary of National Biography.*
3 Private information.

Leslie Hunter

Leslie Stannard Hunter (1890–1983), Bishop of Sheffield, was born in Glasgow on 2 May 1890, the younger son and younger child of John William Hunter, a Congregational minister at Trinity Congregational Church in Glasgow, and his wife, Marian Martin, formerly of Hull. J. W. Hunter was a liberal preacher, concerned for women's rights, and of considerable civic influence. Educated at Kelvinside Academy, and from 1909 at New College, Oxford, Leslie Hunter obtained a second-class honours degree in theology in 1912. He spent time in France with the YMCA in 1916, and also became a friend of Baron von Hügel, growing to admire his liberal Catholicism and mysticism. His elder brother was killed in the First World War.

Charles Gore confirmed Hunter into the Anglican church in 1913. His first post, as Study Secretary of the Student Christian Movement (SCM; 1913–20), was a decisive influence. After ordination in 1916 he also served part-time curacies in Brockley and St Martin-in-the-Fields (hero-worshipping H. R. L. Sheppard, the vicar) and as a hospital chaplain. He published the first of many books, *The Artist and Religion* (1915), arising from work with students in colleges of art.

In 1919 Hunter married Grace Marion (d. 1975), a Cambridge graduate and SCM staff member, the daughter of Mary and Samuel McAulay, a farmer of Aylesby, Lincolnshire. Her hospitality complemented Hunter's taciturnity, which could alarm visitors. She became a much-respected JP on the Sheffield bench. They had no children.

A Newcastle-upon-Tyne canonry (1922–6) preceded four creative years as vicar of Barking (1926–30). During the Depression Hunter returned to the north as Archdeacon of Northumberland (1931–9), where he became the effective force in the diocese. *A Parson's Job* (1931) argued for a strongly led team ministry approach in growingly secularized communities. In Newcastle he founded the Tyneside Council of Social Service, recruiting the sociologist Henry Mess, and committed himself to bringing the needs of the north-east – unemployment relief and more generous and imaginative policies in health, housing and education – to the attention of the government. He defended the 1936 Jarrow march as a necessary expression of frustration at indifference by government and City. He preached a Sandringham sermon and wrote letters to *The Times* querying establishment attitudes. He forged links with the German church resistance, joined those working to create the World Council of Churches, and led the 'Men, Money, and the Ministry' movement within the Church of England for the sake of a more militant church with new methods of paying and deploying the clergy. Reforms he suggested were later adopted.

As Bishop of Sheffield (1939–62) Hunter transformed the diocese into the most forward-looking and strategy-conscious within the established church. He was haunted by the gulf between workers and the church. He created a team which included Oliver Tomkins, Alan Ecclestone and others who respected his convictions and shared his aims. Trade union leaders were invited to his home, though at first they were prepared to come only at night. He brought in Edward R. Wickham to build a new type of industrial mission, enabling the

Church to meet workers on their own ground in factories and mines. Unfortunately, timorous ecclesiastical authority later modified this industrial mission, making it pietistic rather than pioneering.

Sociologically, Hunter understood the alienation of working-class people and worked tirelessly to alter the restricted attitudes of churchgoers. He helped to found William Temple College, Whirlow Grange Conference Centre, and Hollowford Youth Centre. In the House of Lords he pleaded the cause of German prisoners of war, the need for clean air, and justice in industrial relations. He was deeply disappointed when introverted central church leadership at Lambeth concentrated on canon law. Distrusting narrow ecclesiastical attitudes, he looked forward to a ministry which would include ordained women; in this, as in the range of his concerns, this unassuming man became the heir of Archbishop William Temple. He ordained more than 200 men and also attracted a number of outstanding women and men to the service of the diocese. He was the founder and first inspirer of what became the Board of Social Responsibility at Church House, Westminster. He was one of the originators of Christian Aid, the most effectual ecumenical movement for famine relief.

Short of stature, with piercing eyes, often difficult to hear, Hunter was no orator, but, as a listener with an imaginative and critical approach, he valued and resolutely used episcopal office to relate Christian faith and activity to twentieth-century life. Of his 14 books, the most perceptive is *A Mission of the People of God* (1961). His italic handwriting, often inviting the reader to accept some difficult task, was known as the 'snare of the hunter'. Critics detected Machiavellian skill, but the young appreciated being taken seriously. Honorary degrees (DCL Durham, 1940; DD Lambeth, 1949; LL D Sheffield, 1953; DD Trinity College, Toronto, 1954) indicated the respect in which he was held by universities and policy-makers. The European Bursary Fund, set up in his memory, witnessed to his lifelong interest in Scandinavian and continental Christianity, and his admiration of the Taizé community. Hunter died at York on 15 July 1983.

David Sheppard

Lord Sheppard of Liverpool, who died of cancer aged 75, was Anglican bishop of that city from 1975 to 1997. Earlier, he had been an English county and Test cricketer, and twice captain of the English team.

Many judged him as the jewel in the crown of the bench of bishops. Many hoped that he might succeed Robert Runcie as Archbishop of Canterbury. His down-to-earth ecumenism, especially in his partnership with the Catholic archbishop of Liverpool, the late Derek Worlock, helped to rescue the city from sectarian Anglo-Irish troubles in tense years; although a southerner, he came to be accepted as a Liverpudlian, which was a rare accolade.

His sympathy for those on the margins of society earned him the disapproval of prime minister Margaret Thatcher and some of her cabinet. The Church of England's report *Faith in the City* (1985), of which he was the leading advocate and spokesman, was described by one Conservative minister as Marxist.

No church leader of his time was more respected as a straight-forward and experienced spokesman in the Lords (where he took the Labour whip), in the media, and as chairman of the General Synod Board for Social Responsibility (1991–6).

Sheppard was born in Chelsea, London, the son of a solicitor; his loving parents encouraged his interest in cricket.

Test cricket toughened him. He became more authoritative, without losing warmth and humour. A close friendship with Len Hutton gave him mental resources and the power of aggressive leadership on which he later drew in Liverpool. By facing cricketing dilemmas – the problems of professional and amateur status, his own decisions not to play in apartheid South Africa or on Sundays – Sheppard learned to deal with situations in which he was in a minority.

After ordination in 1953 and a curacy at St Mary's, Islington, he and his wife Grace, whom he had met at Cambridge, worked at the Mayflower Family Centre in Canning Town. He was convinced that only personal friendship, 'doing ordinary things together' rather than high-powered techniques, could communicate the gospel of Christ. He refused offers to become a globe-trotting preacher, and believed in building bridges and arguing things out. He challenged critics of youth irresponsibility to show their 'stickability' in Canning Town, where he and Grace gave time and patient friendship for 12 years.

After a spell as suffragan bishop of Woolwich (1969–75), he was appointed Bishop of Liverpool in 1975. There, he was appalled by the deprivation of the city's poor and marginalized; Conservative minister Michael Heseltine, sent to Liverpool after the Toxteth riots of 1981, was later to describe some areas as a 'disaster which looks beyond retrieving'.

Sheppard led from the front. He supported a curate in Kirkby, David Thomas, who had denounced a corrupt and inept local housing authority. The bishop went to Kirkby and gave an interview in the corridor outside Thomas's flat in a crumbling tower block. He also joined Archbishop Worlock in a protest march over a Dunlop factory closed without consultation with the workforce.

Sheppard and Worlock joined to write *Better Together* (1988), and, with the Free Church leader in Liverpool, John Newton, produced *With Hope in our Hearts* (1994). Their care for the marginalized was at the core of their understanding of faith. Few bishops in Europe achieved such ecumenical cooperation in these years.

Sheppard and Worlock could transcend their differences. They went to South Africa on a fact-finding mission and holiday before the release of Nelson Mandela. Although they disagreed over the question of contraception in developing countries, they still preached joint sermons that they had prepared together. In Liverpool, Sheppard strongly supported the ordination of women (Worlock did not) but this did not impede common worship, and they even led ceremonies in each other's cathedrals.

When visiting Conservative minister Michael Portillo asked Labour city council leader Harry Rimmer in 1991, 'Who speaks for this community?', Sheppard prompted Rimmer to encourage Worlock to reply. An astonished Portillo said: 'I cannot think of any other city in this country which would think of producing a bishop to speak in the name of the community.'

Efforts to tempt the Sheppards southwards failed, not only because of establishment hostility, but because they had dedicated themselves, with a sensitive yet tough persistence, to the Christian cause in Merseyside. Stickability was what mattered to these able and courageous leaders.

To Sheppard's surprise and delight, early in his retirement in 1998, he was made a member of the House of Lords; as bishop he had often spoken there on mass unemployment, housing deprivation and cuts in public services. He believed that freedom for the powerful often deprived those with weaker bargaining positions. As part of the Keep Sunday Special campaign, he opposed the bill for complete deregulation of Sunday trading, and successfully got it modified. He safeguarded religious broadcasting, argued against evangelicals and other groups having their own radio stations, and urged that 'as God in the person of Jesus Christ entered into the thick of life', so the nation should support 'broadcasting not narrow-casting'.

In retirement, he continued to fight rearguard actions against secularization and the exclusion of religious values, supported by many who did not go to church. In his revealing autobiography *Steps along Hope Street* (2002), he reflected on the embarrassment Christians had felt on speaking openly about cohabiting and about homosexual relationships.

He applauded the 1995 report, *Something to Celebrate: Valuing Families in Church and Society*, for abandoning the phrase 'living in sin' and for accepting the many kinds of relationships in modern British society. He continued to press for equal opportunities: 'It's about getting women and black people to the top.'

In his last years in West Kirby, he enjoyed his family and grand-children, learned to paint, and often walked alone along the seashore 'looking back with thankfulness at God's faithfulness in testing situations'.

One of those testing situations happened when Robert Runcie, Archbishop of Canterbury, retired in 1991; many wished for Sheppard to be prised out of Liverpool and sent to Canterbury. Officials were said to have made it known that Sheppard would not be welcome at Downing Street and that a more traditional appointment would be appropriate. Old, unfair criticisms were repeated: that Sheppard had brought politics into sport and Marxism into theology. This wise, creative and experienced leader, so much respected in the non-church world, was lost to the Anglican Communion.

His lifelong practice at facing challenges, forming teams and inspiring through hopeful leadership attracted many; it was a new model for the church in the twenty-first century. He was a rare catholic evangelical with a difference who recognized the changed world in which the gospel must be lived today.

Poul Hartling

Unique among European clergy, Hartling achieved the posts of foreign and prime minister and United Nations High Commissioner for Refugees. He was born and died in Copenhagen (1914–2000), but for seven years from 1978 travelled the world urging spiritual and material help for defenceless refugees.

Low-key, humane and practical, he devoted himself to the Vietnamese boat-people and later to the Afghans in Pakistan during the Russian occupation. He lived his work in the light of his faith, whether having difficult negotiations with Chairman and Mrs Mao, or with some unsympathetic British and French politicians. At the United Nations he was re-elected at the end of his first term by acclamation, and he and his office were honoured with the Nobel Prize.

There was a family tradition of politics, but Hartling was ordained and served as a hospital chaplain, as SCM Secretary and as principal of a teacher training college. He was a sought-after preacher. As a great admirer of England, he spent time at Westcott House, and it was a delight to have such a well-informed European in the seminars. He made lifelong friends with some of his contemporaries, especially Pat Rodger, and in his witty farewell speech to Westcott students revealed his idiomatic skills in being grateful for 'English waistcoats with pockets high and low'. He and his doctor wife Elsbeth were endlessly hospitable to friends throughout their lives.

His wit and determination are revealed in the story of his flight over rugged country as foreign minister when his aircraft was in difficulties. A nervous fellow passenger saw him taking solace in a book, and asked if it was the Bible. 'No,' he replied, 'it's a cookery book. If the aircraft is going down, and we are to be consumed by cannibals, I want to make sure they cook me properly.'

Hartling used his stature and knowledge to remind the nations of their global duties to care for the most unfortunate. He admired the English churchmen William Temple, George Bell and Leslie Hunter, who wanted Christendom to serve a catastrophically wounded world.

When attacked by the American religious right for trying to create 'a welfare world', his spirituality stayed firm. He also admired some English politicians, and welcomed Edward Heath's 'Yes' vote in October 1971 as strengthening Europe's unity, which was important for the Danish people and government. He criticized Western governments who restricted what they called a 'flood' of refugees, and said he had seen a 'whirlwind of suffering'.

His was a Christian voice often ignored, but never failing in intelligent courage.

Leslie Brown

Leslie Brown was one of the last generation of English bishops who gave outstanding service overseas, both to the ecumenical movement and in creating indigenous episcopal leadership in the Anglican Communion.

As a linguist at home in ancient languages and in Malayalam and Luganda, he was able to shape the worship of the Church of South India (CSI), inaugurated in 1947, and to found many of the dioceses of Anglicanism in East Africa. The Eucharist of the Church of South India, and its ordination service, won sympathetic attention in Roman Catholic circles as the preparations for Vatican II were going forward in Europe. The CSI liturgy, with its emphasis on thanksgiving and with the celebrant facing the Christian community and the congregation greeting each other at the Peace, prepared the way for the Anglican revised communion service. Though Brown was slight in build and shy in temperament, he had great influence in the Church in India, East Africa and later in England.

Brown was born in 1912 and brought up in north London, working as a clerk in a City counting house, but giving his real energies to studying Latin and Greek in evening classes and running a Scout group. His call to the ministry led him to St John's, Highbury, an evangelical college, friends in his parish aiding him with fees. Through the Student Christian Movement branch at his college, he became a disciple of Fr Gabriel Hebert of Kelham, the liberal Anglo-Catholic scholar.

Offering himself to the Church Missionary Society, Brown was sent to Kerala and was soon joined by Winifred, his doctor wife, whom he had married in 1939. Their home was in an extremely poor, low-caste village where his wife pioneered social medicine and family planning in dispensaries, and Brown opened churches and schools. Living on local food, they both became ill and were embarrassed when their neighbours, though themselves desperately poor, pleaded with them to eat more expensive food.

After a period of sick leave, Brown was sent to teach at theological colleges, where he trained future ministers of different traditions (Anglican, Methodist, Presbyterian and Baptist) whose friendships later became the foundation of the united Church.

To their total surprise, after 14 years in India, Archbishop Geoffrey Fisher summoned the Browns to work in Uganda. They returned to London and Brown at once started to learn Luganda and prepared to be consecrated bishop. He was much relieved that Southwark was chosen for the service, its fees being lower than those of St Paul's or Westminster!

Once in East Africa, he became involved in the crisis over the exile of the Kabaka by the British administration, itself soon to depart. Brown was a tireless pastor and his wife resumed her medical work. In 1960 he became Archbishop of Uganda, Rwanda and Burundi and travelled widely despite the very unsettled political situations. After his retirement in 1965 he remained committed to Uganda and visited the devastated church after President Idi Amin ordered the murder of Archbishop Janani Luwum.

From 1966 to 1978 Brown was Bishop of St Edmundsbury and Ipswich. He remained sensitive to lay opinion and succeeded in setting up a novel (to Anglicans) pastoral ministry of elders who were recognized as having authority in parishes. Brown was one of the founders of Hengrave Hall, in Suffolk, as an ecumenical centre mainly staffed by Roman Catholics but welcoming members of all the churches. Both he and his wife missed some of the optimism and *joie de vivre* of African Christianity (in Luganda the word for 'hope' is the same as that for 'expect').

Brown was so adaptable that he was sought out for many temporary tasks. He was for a time chaplain both of Downing College and Jesus College, Cambridge, chairman of the body responsible for Anglican ordinands, and a member of the Anglican Consultative Council. He was always resilient; at Downing, finding no one at Communion and only the organ scholar at Evensong, he joined in college activities and visited everyone, even a startled F. R. Leavis.

Brown never lost his sense of humour, and formed an Atheists' Association of those who expressed themselves agnostic. This was supposedly to 'convert' the chaplain but in fact gained him many loyal supporters. His intelligent teaching, preaching and writing – especially *Three Worlds, One Word* (1981) – did much to prevent the Church of England from becoming introverted.

Brown's concern for liturgy, renewal, ecumenism and pastoral care continued despite his increasing blindness and the illness of his beloved Winifred. He was particularly sought after in Cambridge in retirement, by men and women preparing for ordination and by old friends from India and Africa. As a Suffolk parson put it, 'He spoke with us individually. I was always quite at ease, despite his having been an archbishop.' He was a much-valued pastor and his own vulnerable sensitivity endeared him to the pressurized, whether lay or clerical.

Theme 2

WORLD PEACE, JUSTICE AND TOLERANCE

This second group expands the first theme. It explores the need for justice and peace in the world and for toleration, equality and understanding among people of different nations, beliefs and backgrounds as a route towards achieving it. The lives of those, whether famous or obscure, who have worked to bring about reconciliation and justice in difficult and daunting circumstances point a way forward for future positive action.

Politicians as peacemakers

When Britain's mission to rescue the Falkland Islands ended in victory 20 years ago, the government asked for a thanksgiving service. Dr Rowan Williams, as he then was, now Archbishop, was a strong supporter of the Church's controversial decision. In all, about 1,000 lives had been lost, 253 British and the rest Argentinian.

It was agreed that the service should be ecumenical and held at St Paul's, and that Archbishop Runcie, who had been awarded the Military Cross in the Second World War, should be the preacher. Each casualty from the task force was to be represented by three family mourners. The Queen, the royal family and the country's political and military leaders would all attend with hundreds of those who had fought in the South Atlantic.

No religious service has been so publicly discussed, rather than being left to clerical liturgical experts meeting in studies and vestries to organize. An avalanche of advice descended on Lambeth, St Paul's and the editors of newspapers. Some suggested that the keynote should be to sing 'Onward, Christian Soldiers' and 'Fight the Good Fight'. Others emphasized the costly triumph of patriotic and righteous wrath over the evil regime of General Galtieri, responsible not only for oppressing the Falkland Islanders, but for the brutish deaths of thousands of 'disappeared ones'.

Yet others feared jingoism in church, and urged that attention be paid to the Pope's words in Coventry, when the Lord's Prayer had been said in Spanish and the Pope insisted that war 'should have no place on humanity's agenda for the future and belongs to the tragic past'. Some pacifist groups threatened to demonstrate on the steps of St Paul's and to hold an alternative service in Hyde Park.

The 17 lay and clerical members of the planning group met at the Deanery of St Paul's and represented the churches, the Ministry of Defence, the Palace and the musicians both of St Paul's and Kneller Hall. After long discussions of the public's various hopes and fears, they decided that the service should have the themes of Thanksgiving, Remembrance of the Fallen and Reconciliation.

In those days, national services were often led by male voices only, but on this occasion it was arranged that Mrs Robin Goodfellow, Moderator of the United Reformed Church, should read a lesson. The imaginative 'rainbow prayer', written by Dr Kenneth Greet, was welcomed by all.

Despite the posters 'Why I shall not be at St Paul's today', the service on 29 July was deeply serious. Perhaps the numbers of bereaved children, one of whose cries echoed around the dome in the silence between Last Post and Reveille, made the most lasting impression, along with the archbishop's courageous sermon. 'He deserved a bar to his Military Cross,' a Second World War veteran said. A widow, whose flight commander husband was killed with 22 others on HMS *Ardent*, wrote: 'It was hard to believe that a service could promote such sincerity.'

It certainly promoted reconciliation. Grieving parents who saw the service on television came from Buenos Aires to St Paul's and asked for wreaths to be blessed to take back to their Argentine graves. Argentina's most famous man of letters, Jorge Luis Borges, wrote a lament free from jingoism and full of the pity of war.

They would have been friends but they met only once face to face on some too famous islands. And each one was Cain, and each one was Abel. They buried them together. Snow and corruption know them. The deed to which I refer took place in a time we cannot understand.

Prayers and poetry can prepare an atmosphere in which politicians can be peacemakers.

Religion and honesty

Some years ago I made a journey by train for eight or nine hours in India. The carriage was crowded and there was only one other Englishman with me. All the rest were Indians. In their hospitable way, they started to talk. But the subject of the conversation was bitter. It was the massacre at Amritsar in April 1919 when Brigadier-General Dyer felt it his duty to order Gurkhas to fire on a political meeting. The shooting went on for about six minutes. When it was over 379 people, including many women and children, had been killed and another 1,500 wounded. The Indians in the carriage believed, quite wrongly, that it was a deliberate order of Winston Churchill and several of them recounted that they had had relatives killed or wounded in the tragedy.

We talked about this for two hours and then there was a pause. One of them said, rather shyly and greatly to my surprise, 'Do people ever spit in railway carriages in England?' I replied: 'Some people do, but it's unhygienic.' He looked at me and smiled and said, 'I am afraid there are many people in India who spit on the floor of railway carriages.' This admission had an extraordinary effect in releasing the conversation. We were no longer confrontational. We could tell each other how old we were, what work we did, exactly what our salaries were and what our views were on the most detailed matters of religion.

The transformation was caused by the Indian who was able to admit to a foreigner that there were some things wrong with India, after we had admitted responsibility for the vast tragedy of Amritsar, which some today might call an act of terrorism.

In this century, as acts of terrorism sprawl from continent to continent, there is a depressing feeling that most of us cannot influence these hideous events. Perhaps we are wrong here and should see that every small just act or word of honesty about our own culture can change humanity and its religions for the better. But it is not a simple process.

It is right that the book of martyrs in St Paul's should contain the name of Steve Biko, the victim of a cynical and repressive Christian government for many years receiving financial support from the West. Biko had had a Christian education but came to believe that only a new black consciousness, which asserted black rights against white in South Africa, could create a just society.

Eventually Biko turned to the United States to exert the necessary diplomatic and financial pressure. He rebutted the arguments for a gentle approach to the apartheid regime in Pretoria: 'If Washington wants to contribute to a just society in South Africa, it must discourage investment in South Africa. We blacks are perfectly willing to suffer the consequences. We are quite accustomed to suffering.' It was fear of America's power and no doubt dread of Communism which led the Boer regime to give way.

Biko himself died in police custody after torture, one of the victims of state terror against which the United Nations, Amnesty International and other bodies struggled. From the point of view of the West it is a tragic and shameful story. But it needs to be told, not least in churches and cathedrals which proclaim a vision of the human community governed by love and justice. Religious buildings and teaching need to proclaim the truth.

Those in our world tempted to acts of terror as the only means by which they believe they can be heard need to know that society does listen and that suffering and injustice are not forgotten, least of all in places of prayer, meditation and praise to God, the creator of men and women of all cultures and conditions. The New Testament insight about casting out the log in our own eye so that we can see clearly to cast out the mote in our brother's is needed in the geopolitics of our terror-ridden world. That alone will save us from the dialogue of the deaf and release us from the politics of confrontation without understanding.

Religions have a duty to listen, to remember and to be honest about themselves and their own histories because we belong to each other. Their shrines should not be bland, but transforming; witnesses to truth in a world fast becoming bound by an increasingly vicious circle of hate and fear.

John Taylor

John Taylor, who died aged 86, was Bishop of Winchester between 1975 and 1985, chairman of the Church of England Doctrine Commission from 1978 until 1985, and one of the great missionaries of his generation. Convinced that Christians should leave their church boundaries to listen and think much harder, he pleaded with a startled General Synod to 'go into no-man's land, for the strange meeting, as Wilfred Owen would have described it'.

Taylor's God was cosmic and also worshipped by non-Christians. He felt that there were many, like the novelist George Eliot, who saw that God was to be experienced outside the Church.

Yet the gentle thinker was startlingly decisive. As Bishop of Winchester, he agreed to hand over a redundant Southampton church to a Sikh congregation. He quoted Japanese Christians and French Roman Catholic bishops who had allowed non-Christian bodies to take over unneeded churches. He met stiff opposition – better to bulldoze it for a supermarket than to let immigrant non-Christians use the building, was some synod members' view.

Speaking about instability in marriage, he wished the Church had been more forceful about the disgraceful housing and grinding unemployment which put harsh strains on relationships. He criticized the Church Commissioners' African and housing policy. Some felt him too idealistic – but it was an irony that after his retirement, the Church Commissioners lost £800 million on unwise American property investment.

Taylor's father was the vice-principal of Ridley Hall, an evangelical theological college in Cambridge, and went on to be principal of Wycliffe Hall, Oxford, and then Bishop of Sodor and Man. His son was educated at St Lawrence College, Ramsgate; Trinity College, Cambridge; St Catherine's Society (now college) and Wycliffe Hall, Oxford; and London University's Institute of Education.

From 1938 to 1940, John Taylor was curate of All Souls' in London's West End, and curate-in-charge at St Andrew's Church in St Helens, Lancashire, from 1940 to 1943. In 1945, he was appointed warden of Bishop Tucker College in Mukono, Uganda. He saw that African independence, political and religious, should be welcomed by Western Christians.

Back in Britain in 1954, he was a research worker with the International Missionary Council until 1959. He then became African Secretary, and afterwards, General Secretary of the Church Missionary Society until his appointment as Bishop of Winchester.

What struck candidates, clergy and laity in London and Hampshire was his gentle liberality. He believed the media, especially television, gave the gospel new opportunities. His *African Passion Play* was beautifully filmed in the 1950s, and his *Winchester Cathedral Passion and Resurrection* (1981) drew on his skills as an actor and poet.

Taylor was always producing plays and reviews, and publishing books. *The Primal Vision* (1963) had been groundbreaking on African understanding of religion. His other books on Africa, including *The Growth of the Church in Buganda* (1958), and *Christianity and Politics in Africa* (1957), showed a fresh appreciation of how Africans saw and practised faith in the gospel.

His two most influential books, *The Go-Between God* (1972) and *Enough is Enough* (1975), in some ways more visionary than the Church appeared to be, reached a younger generation. The Church's wealth in Britain and the United States – in contrast to much of the Third World – needed the lifestyle plea which Taylor made. His gentleness, humility and artistic gifts fused in this shy and prophetic thinker.

Norwich and the Ugandan Asians

In 1972, Idi Amin, the tyrannical ruler of Uganda, who was to assassinate so many critics, including the Anglican archbishop, ordered the expulsion of all Ugandan Asians. The Indian community of many thousands had been encouraged under British rule and had given a lead in the construction and maintenance of the railway, and much commercial life. Many of the vast coffee, tea and sugar plantations on the shores of Lake Victoria were owned, financed and managed by Indians. Idi Amin aimed at establishing the popularity of his regime by throwing out all Indians and allowing them to remove little of their property, transferring it all to Ugandan nationals.

Most Ugandan Asians had British passports and Edward Heath's Conservative government rightly offered them asylum in the UK. Dr Donald Coggan, then Archbishop of York, welcomed the government's decision and named Norfolk as one of the counties which might accommodate them. But at once there was a storm of protest in the correspondence columns of the local press. I quote from the flood of letters in the local press and also much personal correspondence:

I hope the suggestion of absorbing Asian immigrants does not materialise. So far Norwich has been free from an immigration problem. ... Once a coloured community moves in, a ghetto is created. ... May I ask how many Asians and coloured the Archbishop and the Dean will house in their own spacious dwellings and also all our MPs and other dignitaries of England, who have vast acres of land. We hear so much from these people yet they never act on their own or give a lead.

If the Asians come to Norwich let them live in the Close and work in the Close. Would the Dean of Norwich welcome them then? Do this fine city of Norwich and Norfolk want to become a Leicester or Bradford or Birmingham? ... Refusing to have Asians here will cause far less suffering than they would experience if they are brought here and we then have to turn them out, as we would do at the first opportunity. Enoch Powell must be accepted as our leader before long, and in the meanwhile no immigrants in Norwich under any circumstances.

I should like to say that there is one 'citizen of Norwich' who will be happy to see Asians here. I spend six months of the year in Leeds where there is a coloured 'ghetto' and I have worked with coloured people and it is no better and no worse than working with English people. . . . How many of your readers have cause to be grateful to 'coloured' doctors and nurses? . . . The Church has much property in the Close and in cranky rectories. Surely it can show practical help by actually housing some of these Asians?

I happen to like Norwich the way it is today and have no wish to see it turned into another problem city. . . . Asians belong in Asia along with their own kind. . . . Alan Webster should give some thought to alleviating some of the many problems such as housing, unemployment and a better standard of living for old-age pensioners. . . . In Norwich we have married couples with children unable to obtain decent accommodation and yet the city is supposed to find homes for people who neither belong here nor are wanted here. If any of the displaced Asians do eventually come to Norwich perhaps the Dean will offer accommodation for at least one family at the Deanery.

Ultimately central and local planning got to work. The government used a Suffolk RAF station as a staging point. The Lord Mayor of Norwich, Dick Seabrook, held a meeting at the City Hall and also visited the Deanery. It was agreed that immediate accommodation should be provided in the Close and the Ugandan Asian family invited became friends with many who live there. Members of this Asian family have given considerable service to the City, both as teachers and as a postmaster. St Mary's Baptist Church and other Christian churches both in the city and the countryside also found accommodation and new friends amongst the expelled Ugandan Asians. Many Norwich people in the 1990s came as happy invited guests to large Asian weddings on Saturdays in St Andrew's Hall. In those years one of Norwich's most respected Lord Mayors was a Jewish refugee from persecution in Central Europe. Norwich has become a 'fine city' in a new sense, where a thoughtful and planned welcome can be given to refugees in the twenty-first century, as was given to so many Huguenots fleeing religious persecution as Protestants in earlier days. Our experience was that frank and open discussion could eventually lead to agreement and effective action.

Prayer versus dogma

When Baron Friedrich von Hügel gave a friend a copy of Julian of Norwich's *Revelations of Divine Love*, he wrote in his gift: 'This shewed our good Lord, to make us glad and merry.'

Von Hügel (1852–1925), an influential Roman Catholic thinker and writer although he remained a layman, was always suspicious if religion was depressing or clinging to formulae, or finicky or fastidious.

'I used to wonder in my intercourse with John Henry Newman, how one so good . . . could be so depressing,' he wrote. 'I used to marvel contrariwise, in my intercourse with the Abbé Huvelin, how one more melancholy in natural temperament than even Newman himself, could so radiate spiritual joy.'

It was the Abbé Huvelin (1835–1910) who shared such joy with von Hügel and the thousands of visitors over the years who came to his darkened room in Paris. They felt that, in a unique sense, Huvelin was open to them and convinced them that they were not completely alone in the world. 'Prayer will be for you rather a state than a precise deliberate act,' he used to teach them, and they experienced it with him.

Many Britons in France have felt this shared spiritual joy and unargumentative generosity. British civilians left during the war in Dinard – in German hands after 1940 – found their faith deepened when, each Sunday in St Bartholomew's Anglican church, a French Catholic priest celebrated for them in English the Book of Common Prayer service of Holy Communion without asking questions. The same church was also used on several occasions during the war by Lutheran soldiers of the German army.

In the 1960s in the Dordogne a hurricane demolished an international holiday camp; the village opened its hall free of charge to all those whose tents had been wrecked. We responded by joining a blood-donor session in the village school (and found the post-session red wine and cold ham much more reinvigorating than their British equivalents).

When the *curé* discovered that I was an Anglican clergyman he insisted that I shared in the consecration of the Mass on Sunday. To my questions about the bishop and regulations, he replied, 'If the Bishop of Tulle knew he would be delighted.'

I was of use to this fine priest by completing the end of the Mass while he set off for Clermont-Ferrand hospital, at breakneck speed on a motorbike, to visit a sick firefighter.

Today the shortage of priests in many small towns and villages in France means that there cannot be a service every Sunday. French clergy sometimes ask Anglican clergy to fill the gaps.

On the holiday festival of the Assumption, an important event in Brittany, an Anglican with many friends in the French church was invited by the *curé*, who had to be elsewhere that day, to take his place. As he has fluent French (he had done his National Service with French troops clearing German minefields) he could save the situation and he communicated more than 800 at this Mass. As a teacher as well as a priest and musician, he occasionally brings a church choir with him. He also finds himself much in demand to describe how English Christians face the same problems, and he shares the Anglican liturgy with fellow believers across the Channel.

Another Anglican chaplain visiting a French jail with many English prisoners is warmly welcomed as a colleague by a French Catholic priest, and they reinforce each other's ministry. Fortunately, both these Anglican priests had trained at Lincoln Theological College, where there was often a Catholic priest on the staff.

In the 1970s a cardinal, desperate for a priest, asked an Anglican to celebrate the All Saints Mass in a small village. When the Anglican protested that he was an Anglican, the cardinal replied: 'The question of Anglican orders is a very open one, and they (the villagers) will love it.'

When in the winter there was sometimes no Anglican priest for the English community's Christmas Eucharist, an English-speaking French Roman Catholic priest used to celebrate a Christmas Eucharist strictly according to the Book of Common Prayer. Often French clergy are animated by a spirit of cooperative friendliness more than by sticking to the rules – prayer seems to them to matter most.

A London couple who, in retirement, decided to join the half-a-million or so British with homes in France, chose the tiny village of Maxou, well off the beaten track north of Cahors.

The Romanesque village church opposite was receiving a government restoration as they worked in their house and garden.

When the restoration was finished this beautiful church remained locked. The British couple persuaded the authorities to entrust them with the key, and the *curé*, who had nearly 20 villages in his care, became a trusting friend.

It seems to be a matter of course that these Anglicans are welcomed at Mass, for it is they who have made the church accessible and organized recitals of music at weekends.

When they returned to England for a family Christmas they arranged for the church to be floodlit even though, owing to the shortage of clergy, there were no services.

In many communities such quiet cooperation leads to grassroots ecumenism, sharing life's needs, troubles and joys.

To quote the Abbé Huvelin again in some words he gave to von Hügel: 'Our Lord won the world not by his fine speeches ... it is necessary to act. Have no fear; act, love, you have an infinite need for expansion; constraint will kill you.'

Gonville ffrench-Beytagh

Wandering down Cheapside before dawn, to take the accounts of St Paul's Cathedral to Mansion House – the then Lord Mayor was a keen member of the Church and an expert on bankruptcy – I noticed a light from an open door. It was not another City crime, but Gonville ffrench-Beytagh already at prayer. It was typical of this most human priest that his late evenings of parties, companionship and science fiction began so early at his prayer desk and altar – the far side of which he believed was in heaven.

Gonville ffrench-Beytagh was the most famous Anglican dean of the twentieth century. His upbringing was bizarre: born in Shanghai, where his father was a lapsed Irish Catholic seminarian turned cotton company director, and his mother mostly away, he was brought up by French and Japanese servants. Alcohol, money and sex were always problems for his family.

His mixed-up boyhood was exacerbated by a spell of school at Monkton Combe which led him to vow never to enter a church again, though the chant of *Nunc dimittis* stayed in his subconscious. Bristol Grammar School did better as he had a talent for sport, especially as a scrum-half, but he graduated as a tramp in New Zealand and as a clerk in a Johannesburg mining machinery firm with a hefty account in the office labelled 'Bribery and Corruption'. Via Tubby Clayton, Alan Paton and Bishop Geoffrey Clayton and a cathedral midnight communion he was ordained, but 'putting on a dog collar made me feel rather a fool'. The Jewish girl with whom he was going out at the time just rocked and rocked with laughter. Gonville admitted that he never got round to being married.

Appointed Dean of Salisbury, Rhodesia, in 1955 and ten years later Dean of Johannesburg, he found the apartheid policy terrifying. South Africa, he said, was ruled by 'the whip and the gun'. Guilty that he had done so little over the failure of partnership in the Federation of Central Africa, he plunged into concern over black injustice. He was not a 'political' clergyman nor a publicity seeker, but so tragically experienced, alert and affectionate that he felt bound to take a stand against the 'South African way of death', as he described the slow descent into racial conflict.

He described his arrest, interrogation and trial in 1971–2 in his able autobiography *Encountering Darkness* (1973). In his historic trial his largely Jewish defence team succeeded in limiting the scope of the Terrorism Act, one of the signs that the tide was beginning to turn after the low water marks of the imprisonment of Mandela and the massacre at Sharpeville. The dean received world sympathy and support, especially from the United States.

Gonville was not tortured, but he suffered deeply during the Security Police eight-day interrogation. Shouted abuse ('You don't preach Christianity, you preach shit') followed by intense questioning on associates and suppliers of money led to difficult soft-sell periods over a cup of tea ('Surely you know sexual relationships between black and white are forbidden in the Bible ... a man may not mix his seed with that of an animal'). Visits from the British consul, his doctors, his Prayer Book sent by his bishop, and self-administration of Holy Communion in coffee drugged by his captors were moments of light in an experience which was always to haunt him. The hopes of those concerned with human liberty round the world and the prayers of the worldwide Church seemed to get through, though he knew nothing of them at the time.

On his acquittal his defence team urged him to leave South Africa to avoid further harassment by the Security Police and possible physical violence from the right wing. Free but feeling inwardly guilty, he arrived in London to find a suspicious establishment wondering if he was a semi-terrorist. Once again he had to search for work.

East Anglia, proud of other stirrers such as Oliver Cromwell and Edith Cavell, offered him a house and a chaplaincy at Norwich Cathedral. The Norfolk legal fraternity restaged his trial in a crowded public hall. However, he preferred to accept a curacy in Westminster (to the derision of his South African critics) and in 1974 became Rector of St Vedast. He retired in 1987 to Tredegar Square, where he lived with a small community of friends led by Alison Norman, who cared for him to the end.

His last public service was to examine his own experience of depression and to be one of the few guides to write openly of the black depths, including suicide. He recognized his own repressed rage, hypersensitivity to failure and sense of rejection. He knew how often Christian leaders refuse to face conflict because they will not face the tensions in themselves, analysing their own 'hardness of heart'. He urged depressives to 'sort out some solid reasons why you should not commit suicide'. His book *Facing Depression* (1978) is widely used. To the very end he endeavoured to gain something from the dark side of life and to share his own conviction of God's concern for the lonely (see *A Glimpse of Glory*, 1986).

Gonville was the despair of ecclesiastical organizers and tidy archdeacons. He was very traditional in worship, as if the 1928 South African Prayer Book had dropped from heaven. But his world experience led him to attack the soft and the insular in London Christianity. In the eighties he could still swing the vote at a City meeting where clerical fogies were determined to condemn the World Council of Churches.

He knew at his desk and his altar his good luck at having been spared the fate of Steve Biko. He remembered how the Afrikaner women and children had suffered in the British concentration camps during the Boer War. He never forgot those in prison confined either by bars or by blackness. His jokes, his laughter, his drinks, the confusion of his study and his silences, as well as his personal caring, will live on in the memories of many in Africa and London.

A fusion of the spiritual and the secular

An East Anglian sixth form was discussing the horrendous news from America and local reactions. 'My parents are in anguish,' said a Muslim girl. Their mosque had been daubed with abuse and they were fearful for themselves. 'We are all British citizens,' the girl went on, 'and my brothers if called up would certainly fight against terrorists.' She said her family felt aghast at being blamed for the unspeakable tragedy.

One of the prayers at the national memorial service in St Paul's spoke of nations 'bleeding from the unhealed wounds of their history'. We are one of those nations, and we should cherish those occasions when our different stories and convictions, secular, religious and political, can be shared, sometimes despite the efforts of administrations who insist on separation.

Britain abounds in societies which are secular and religious at once. Both the Samaritans and Oxfam were founded by Church of England parsons, but their thousands of supporters are not required to repeat any creed. The hundreds of volunteers who have given weeks of their summer in Cathedral Camps, bagging pigeon droppings in ecclesiastical roofs, have not been asked to read the Thirty-Nine Articles.

Now that cold winds have arrived and summer has slipped away, it is worth remembering some of the achievements of these societies which fuse the spiritual and the matter of fact.

Trying to be aware of the details, sounds and smells of a summer garden in Bergh Apton, Norfolk, I found inscribed on a slate seat in a shady corner some words by John Keats: 'And then there crept a little noiseless noise among the leaves, born of the very sigh that silence leaves.'

Places where you are welcomed for a day of silence can now be found on all five continents thanks to the generosity and vision of home-owners who have formed the Movement for Quiet Gardens. The counsellor who led our brief retreat began one of her prayers with the phrase: 'Explorer God'. Encouraged to be seekers, we were blessed with a feeling of liberation and encouraged to respond, in a setting of growth and beauty, with a radical and liberal mind not hostile to our own traditions but not railroaded by them.

Not far away there is an annual commemoration of the Burston School Strike, predominantly a political and secular occasion. But in the speeches on the green another open-air moment, the Sermon on the Mount, is often recalled. The strike, now about 100 years ago, was sparked off by the sacking of the village headmistress by the school governors with the rector in the chair. The head was a devout and brilliant teacher but her husband championed poorly paid farm workers. The village built a 'strike school' on the green and received support from trade unions.

Today a procession with banners along the route of the parents and their children is followed yearly through the fields. Amnesty International is one of the many causes represented on the green: the spirit of fighters for righteousness, from the prophet Amos to the martyr Oscar Romero, can be felt in this festival in the countryside.

Between Bergh Apton and Burston lies Rockland St Mary. Here two retired teachers have become couriers for aid journeys between the twinned cities of Norwich and Novi Sad, Serbia. The journeys can be demanding. Getting a bulky DNA sequencer through Hungarian customs was tricky, but the Serbian scientists were immensely grateful for this gift from the John Innes Institute.

Elsewhere, an East Anglian water company has helped to fit a water supply across the Danube, and there are youth exchange programmes. The Novi Sad–Norwich prayer used by Christians, Muslims, Jews and humanists alike expresses their hopes: 'Lead me from death to life, from falsehood to truth, from despair to hope, from war to peace. Let peace fill our hearts, our world, our Universe.'

The achievements of these small groups this summer, whether engaging in the struggle for justice, or forging international links, can endure through clouded days and help to liberate dark minds and cold places.

Working together

Hardly a day passes without some report on the BBC news of bloody violence and conflict somewhere in the world.

Such hostilities contrast with the idealist motto of the BBC itself: 'Nation shall speak peace unto nation'. This is not a prophecy gleaned from some sacred religious scripture, but was written in 1927 by one of the first BBC governors, as though he had foreseen the world trials of the twenty-first century.

When the sixtieth anniversary of the BBC was celebrated in London at St Paul's Cathedral in 1982, care was taken to invite distinguished religious leaders, Hindu, Buddhist, Sikh, Muslim, Jewish and Christian, to pray for 'the peace of the faiths'. The imam G. M. A. Sulaiman prayed: 'O Allah, thou art peace and from Thee comes peace. Bless us with peace and admit us into the abode of peace.'

Artists sometimes speak peace more compellingly than others with a public voice. Antony Gormley's *Angel of the North*, the largest statue of our days – it is 20m (65ft) tall, nearly 60m (197ft) wide and weighs 208 tonnes – is not beautiful; its wings are weathered and rusty-brown, but it can resist howling gales and it stands on deep foundations in rock above a 200-year-old coal mine. It bears comparison with those other northern masterpieces of communication, the Tyne Bridge and Durham Cathedral.

When first unveiled, the *Angel* was subject to vitriolic criticism ('brash', 'wicked', 'banal') from those who believed that only housing and industry deserved to be built. In contrast a young Gateshead girl sang its praises and confessed how proud it made her to live in the North, opening its arms in welcome. As travellers rush past it, northwards and southwards along the A1, it reminds many of them of hope and the Spirit.

The *Angel* has many different interpretations. To some it is an enlightened Icarus; to some simply a landmark for rail and road travellers, and to some Christians it is a reminder of Christ opening wide his arms, a symbol of hope and resurrection. As an angel it can speak to many spiritualities – Christian, Jewish, Muslim, Eastern and humanist. To all it suggests something beyond.

One organizer of the deadly July bombings in London lived in Leeds and was a British Muslim. It is appropriate that a Yorkshire and Humber Faiths Forum has been created (New York, which suffered its own attacks, has one of the oldest interfaith centres). The forum discusses complex questions that matter hugely. Muslims, Jews and Christians alike care about Iraq, about Israel and Palestine, about the economies of developing countries. People who care about faith need to be able to speak to each other and listen to each other. The religious and cultural dimensions of British culture today require us to change.

I read theology at Oxford but I never read the Qur'an nor did I ever imagine that the Yorkshire church where I first celebrated Holy Communion would one day belong to a non-Christian group. Now we all need a wider horizon.

The phrase 'British Muslim' was coined by the late Sir Zaki Badawi, knighted in 2004 for his eirenic work. He was consulted by the Archbishop of Canterbury before the foundation of the Christian–Muslim Forum, launched at Lambeth Palace in January this year. Rowan Williams, Archbishop of Canterbury, said: 'This is not about elites. This is about ordinary people working together on the needs and challenges that face us all. Faith is a perfectly normal activity for human beings.'

The prime minister said at the Lambeth launch: 'The need has never been greater . . . The greater the knowledge the greater the understanding, the greater the understanding the greater the respect.'

Since humanity must learn to listen and think, as well as speak, such meeting places are crucial. These small ventures in Leeds and London may begin to enable the religious to hear each other and so to speak peace.

More than conquerors

I don't think we Christians have understood what carrying the Cross means. We are not carrying the Cross when we are poor or sick or suffering small everyday things – these are all part of life. The Cross comes when we try to change things. That is how it came for Jesus.

In these words, Fr Miguel d'Escoto, then Nicaraguan foreign minister (in 1986), spoke of the sufferings common to Central and South America among those who had become convinced that their task *as Christians* is to join in the struggle to change things. During the last century, the former Spanish possessions have attained independence, but in most cases, they are under the control of the local land-owning army classes. The transfer of power from Europe has left the *campesinos* and the urban working classes without a real share in the life of their country. During the next hundred years, there will be a slow transfer, but the process is painful and frequently bloody. In England, where our political and religious revolution took place in the seventeenth century, we have, deep in our history, the traditions which should enable us to sympathize with the hard choices, and frequently the hard fate, which is the lot of our fellow Christians in Central and South America.

In 1985 I was asked to lead a small group sent by the English churches in London to be alongside the sufferers in Guatemala, El Salvador and Nicaragua. Our report was published under the title *More than Conquerors*. It was a searing and dangerous experience to share with those who had often been on death lists and may be on death lists again, to be alongside women political and religious prisoners and to visit the holy places where so recently men and women, sometimes very young, had met their death. As a result of our visit, we were able to celebrate in Westminster and St Paul's cathedrals the sixth anniversary of the assassination on 24 March 1980 of Archbishop Oscar Romero in the hospital chapel in San Salvador.

Oscar Romero was appointed Bishop of San Salvador on the recommendation of the government as a thoroughly conservative, non-political bishop. He had served in the outlying town of San Miguel, where he acquired a reputation for being quiet, pastoral and not prepared to make any statements on the struggle for greater

political freedom. He was brought, like another Thomas Becket, to
the capital and there the fate of the poor, the tortures and the rapes
by the Treasury Police under government orders, 'conscientized'
him. He began to demand that the government should stop burning the forests, bombing the guerrillas, and using helicopters to
kill their opponents. He even appealed to President Carter. Whereas
he had been totally committed to private Catholic spirituality, he
accepted his position as leading bishop in a country suffering from
civil war and finally appealed to the soldiers to stop shooting the
rebels. That was the day before his death. A marksman shot him at
the altar and, as one of his friends said, a mouthful of blood was
his final word to his Church and his country.

His tomb in the south transept dominates the cathedral in San
Salvador, and a stream of pilgrims flows round it. Close beside, there
is a banner to the 'Four Roses of December', four young Catholic
women shot by the army close to the international airport. Because
the young, both young women and young men, are so committed
to God in the here and now, they must often suffer more than the
cautious elderly men.

Another makeshift banner hangs beside the scene, proclaiming in
Spanish the words that are so true and yet so costly:

> The light shines in the darkness and the darkness cannot put
> it out.

Being a martyr in Central America comes suddenly upon people,
young or old, teenagers or parish priests. This letter from Fr John
Medcalf, whom I met in February of this year, describes how he
found things in Nicaragua in November 1985. Life has been even
more dangerous since, but perhaps one letter gives the impression
of the reality and suddenness of martyrdom more clearly than sum-
marized extracts.

> I write this letter in the fond hope that it may arrive before the
> situation becomes desperate.
>
> After less than a month in Nicaragua, I find myself in Cristo
> Redentor Parish, in a small town called Muelle de los Bueyes (means:
> Ox-ford, but there are no university spires) on the chief link road
> between the Pacific and Atlantic oceans.
>
> In the last week, this area has become the main focus of combat
> between the local Sandinista army and the US-backed 'contras'. This

parish house may well be turned into a casualty hospital within a day or so.

Last Sunday I was scheduled to say Mass at 2 pm in the village of Cara de Mono, but the 'contras' got there first. At 12.30 pm about 100 heavily armed 'contra' mercenaries burst out of the tropical rain forest and tried to capture the village. There was heavy cross-fire immediately behind the Catholic chapel, and the first to die was Ivan Torres, a 17-year-old villager fighting with the Sandinistas. From the parish house here in Muelle, only 10 km from Cara de Mono, we clearly heard the machine-gun fire. Fr Jose Cuercio (the parish priest) and myself reached that village at 3.30 and discovered that the mercenaries had been driven off; 19 of them had been killed and many others severely wounded. The Sandinista Air Force had sent in 3 small reconnaissance planes and 2 troop-carrier helicopters, and the village resembled an outsized wasp nest. My most poignant memory of that Sunday afternoon was the horrific grief of the young brothers of Ivan Torres, whose head had been blown off by a grenade.

The village catechist ('delegate of the Word' is the official title here in Central America) is a woman who also belongs to the Sandinista Police. She described how her house was surrounded by a group of 'contras' and how she repelled the attack single-handed with a sub-machine gun. Her prompt action must have saved the village from a blood-bath. The high morale and great bravery of Nicara-guans like Rosa Maria is what distinguishes the Sandinista cause at the present time.

Since the 'contra' attack on Sunday afternoon, there have been reports of a build-up of forces on both sides. One of the 6 parish deacons came in yesterday to the parish house; 80 mercenaries had passed within a few yards of his smallholding. His fear was all the more understandable when I learned that his teenage daughter was taken hostage to Costa Rica a few months ago, where she was repeatedly raped before eventually escaping. Another of our Deacons is on a 'contra' blacklist. Because of his adherence to the Sandinista militia, his house has been burned once, and there have been 2 attempts on his life.

In many ways we are living from one day to the next without a clear vision of the way things will work out. The massive involvement of the USA in trying to destroy what it regards as Communism is yet another major error on the part of the Reagan administration. The silence and compliance of most of the Nicaraguan Bishops is perhaps no worse than the performance of the German Bishops when faced with Nazism 50 years ago, but it is equally unpalatable.

I had the luck to talk with John Medcalf during his 205-mile march, the Lenten Via Crucis (Way of the Cross), from the northern Honduran border of Nicaragua, along the mountain road with bridges destroyed by the Contras, down on to the hard, hot American highway to the capital. The march lasted 15 days and the 120 people who made the entire journey were joined by hundreds, and then thousands, of men, women and children. Seven men did the entire Way of the Cross in their wheelchairs, just a few of the thousands of war-wounded in Nicaragua. At times we were welcomed like a liberation army. Towards the end of the journey, two priests shut the doors of their churches to the pilgrims, but peasant sacristans countermanded their clergy and no doubt lost their jobs for opening their doors to the church of the poor.

When Holy Week was over, they had time to remember Ivan Torres, the 17-year-old killed in the battle. Illiteracy in Nicaragua is treated like a disease – to be eliminated as quickly and as painlessly as possible. So a library was erected in the village of Caro de Muno, and opened on Sunday, 6 April 1986. His mother gave a little speech before cutting the pink ribbon across the doorway:

> My son is living still. I know it. He is living with us, especially in this small library which has grown out of his dead body. If I could give birth to more sons like Ivan, to die for our revolution, I would gladly, gladly do it.

So the villagers cheered and clapped and wept. The building only cost £250 and about the same sum to fit out with basic books about agriculture and first aid and children's stories and a dictionary and a Bible. Other villages have seen this village library and are asking for their own. You don't need sermons about life and death. It is all for real. Holy Week had the bonfires blazing outside the churches on Holy Saturday. Four days earlier, a group of Contras had captured a Catholic catechist, Donato Mendoza, in his home. He was castrated, blinded, tortured and then shot. Three days later, as it happened, on Good Friday, his mutilated body was found. He had always worn a chain and cross because of his position in the Church as catechist. He had lost the cross working in the fields a few days before. It was this chain without a cross that identified his dead, mutilated body. As a Catholic nun who described all this said: 'He no longer wore a cross of metal. His life had taken on the passion and death of Jesus.'

So, Easter Day came and they celebrated Mass with Donato's family – mother, brother, sister, wife, nine children, two grandchildren. On the altar was the chain matted with blood and dirt. There was no cross. The service reflected their faith that as Christ's life did not terminate on the cross but in the victory of the resurrection, so they believed that Donato had conquered death and suffering and lives on by the power of the same God whom he served faithfully during the 40 years of his life, many of them as a village catechist.

There are many martyrs in emerging countries who spend years in prison. Edward Torre spent eight years in President Marcos's prisons in the Philippines before he was liberated by Mrs Aquino. In the women's political prison in El Salvador, we met those fine women leaders who had been supporting the Popular Movement. Sometimes they were snatched from cafés in the capital. Police vehicles with smoked darkened windows tour the streets watching for figures believed to be in touch with the insurgents. After a long talk with one of these women in the prison, I said: 'Whose is the baby?' (She had told me she had been in prison for a year.) 'Oh,' she replied, 'I was raped by one of the guards.' She was smart, well dressed, with a little jewellery, and the baby on her knee was well looked after. The discipline in the women's prisons, the rows of neatly stacked washing, the coffee so carefully made for visitors, the powerful poster which the guards have been compelled to allow them to leave up on the walls of their room, all speak about women committed to the struggle. The struggle is dire. 'Never on our knees except to take aim,' a motto I found on one of the posters, hints at the horrors of civil war.

Ought Christians to be so identified with such a grim struggle? Central America is harsh. Most skylines seem to have a volcano in the distance with gentle but threatening smoke. The centre of Managua was destroyed by an earthquake. The sense of menace greets the visitor at many an airport. Piles of bombs and the gunship helicopters lie beside the runways. The Christians who are committed to these harsh wars believe that those who become leaders at the end of a revolutionary process are usually amongst those who have fought longest and hardest. As Salvador Samayoa of El Salvador said:

> If there are comrades who are Christians, then we will have Christian leaders. But if the Christians don't accompany us, then there won't be Christian leaders.

The Governor General of Belize was present recently at a service in St Paul's for the Order of St Michael and St George. She told me how many are fleeing from Guatemala and El Salvador through the forests of her country, and what problems this creates. Guatemala has some of the 'killing fields' of Central America. Democracy is struggling but basically, control is by 'bullets and beans'. Just below the surface there is agony. There was a plot of flowers in front of a widow's little house. 'Why do you grow flowers there?' someone asked. 'That's where they killed my husband,' she replied. They forced open the door and fired 12 shots. The Methodist pastor stayed beside her and gave her what relief he could. All she had was faith and memory and a little plot of flowers.

One village catechist explained to me, in a refugee camp close to the Guasapa volcano, where a major drive was being made by government troops, that he had hidden his notes on the Gospel of St Luke, carefully wrapped up in polythene, and he knew the location of the tree where they were hidden. 'When I go back,' he said, 'I shall find them and start my work as catechist again.' He looked very old. Probably the stress of life in an insurgency area, with most of his family fighting, has aged him prematurely and he may have been under 40. Words, even had I had Spanish, would have been inadequate. All one could do was to embrace, and the feel of his stubbly, bony, firm but battered face stays with me today.

In the old terminology, martyrs are simply witnesses. If we wonder whether the Christian faith is for real, or simply words and gestures endlessly repeated in synods and conferences by ecclesiastical groups struggling to outwit each other, we should not desert the church of our fathers, but rather remember the church of our contemporaries across the oceans. They are not separated from the reality of Christ. Neither tribulation nor anguish, nor persecution, nor famine, nor nakedness nor the sword, can destroy them. No, in all these things, they are *more than conquerors* through him who loves them and whose life they proclaim through their own courageous witness, sometimes unto death, and always to resurrection. Our London ecumenical group which I had the privilege to lead in Central America included a Jesuit and a sister of a Catholic order, all working together and visiting on our way home the State Department in Washington and the US ambassador in London. Fortunately today USA policy towards Central America is more liberal and tolerant.

Theme 3

OPENING UP THE CHURCH

One of the great developments of the twentieth century has been the opening up of the Anglican Church to new challenges and areas for action. Two in particular are represented here. One is the opportunity for fuller involvement of women in the Church. Another is the vital issue of engagement with the problems of urban society. This chapter considers these challenges and shows how cathedrals can participate in them.

Julian of Norwich

On 8 May 1373 – the third Sunday after Easter – a woman who described herself as 'simple and unlettered' had an overwhelming experience. The result was the *Revelations of Divine Love*, the first book written in English by a woman. Her style is vivid and energetic, using both French and Anglo-Saxon words, confident that the search for God can be shared by all. Today, Julian of Norwich is not only the most popular English mystic, but also the most controversial.

Printed editions and commentaries now appear in many languages. There are Julian groups, informal and domestic, meeting in Britain, France, America and Japan. Her 600th anniversary in May 1973 brought a large pilgrimage to her shrine in Norwich. At the cathedral beforehand, Catholics and Protestants, habited monks and nuns and young people from many countries, joined in conference, eucharist and procession. A group of French nuns gathered the rose petals drifting down from the clerestory after the Blessing and put them in their missals as if they were sentimental relatives at the wedding of a beloved daughter in their own family.

Women Against the Ordination of Women has now put out a pamphlet, *Mother Julian: A Woman Betrayed* (by Elaine Bishop), which argues that Julian has been hijacked and that impious hands have been laid upon her. The author complains that Julian's words, set to music by Alan Wilson, were sung in Westminster Abbey in the presence of a former Archbishop of Canterbury on the fortieth anniversary 'of the so-called priesting of the Chinese woman Li Tim Oi'. She argues that Julian's stress on the 'motherhood of God' and on 'praying to Christ as to our mother as well as to our father' has also been 'betrayed' by those women who ask that Holy Orders should no longer be barred to them simply because they are women.

Far from being 'betrayed', the growing popularity of Julian as a writer to whom 'we can scurry', as Sir Alec Guinness puts it, suggests that when we think of God as mother and pray to Jesus Christ as our mother as well as our brother, our prayers are strengthened by current Jungian hypotheses. She did not feminize Christ; she insisted that the feet of Christ were covered by 'mirk'. For all the joy she experienced at thinking of God's love seen in the life of his son, she was fully alert to his hideous rejection and final crucifixion amongst terrorists. The ambiguous word 'feminist' can do an injustice to women and men who draw strength from Julian's insights on the motherhood of God.

Julian was subversive in the sense that she found some aspects of the organized post-Constantinian church deeply questionable. The Bishop of Norwich of her time led his troops in battle against dissident peasants and took part in the trial and was present at the hanging, drawing and quartering of one of their leaders. Living close to Norwich Castle, Julian's pilgrimage of the mind contrasted with this the overflowing love of God which alone could hold together her world fragmented by war, plague and religious divisions.

Perhaps there is a trace of the artful in Julian's simplicity, as if she would persuade us into a more profound faith without openly challenging the high orthodoxy of the officials. She drew on the sights of the city, the countryside and the shore, and her symbol of the hazelnut has been described by Ronald Blythe as 'one of the most inspired written concepts of the divine love since St Paul'.

The Bible, Platonic mysticism and her own experience are her sources in describing the human pilgrimage. If she was heretical in believing that all shall be saved, this suggests that she is the selective hijacker who has enough verve to choose what she finds to be true from a number of sources.

Today, Julian speaks beyond the boundaries of Christendom about those questions which tease everyone, whether Christians or not. Laying impious hands on her ideas only occurs when our nerve fails, when we shrink from embracing her divine energy and optimism. When women are recognized as priests in the Church of England and the Church then applies itself to the deepest problems of faith and its relations with other religions, this joyous mystic will be recognized as belonging to everyone, pointing to a universal source of hope.

Florence Tim Oi Li

Florence Li was the first Anglican woman priest, a religious leader of distinction and compelling simplicity.

In 1984 she read the Gospel in Chinese at a eucharist in Westminster Abbey which was also a thanksgiving for the fortieth anniversary of her ordination to the priesthood. Her original orders had been rejected by two English archbishops, William Temple and Geoffrey Fisher, and by the 1948 Lambeth Conference. Now, 40 years later, in a packed abbey, standing room only, the former Archbishop Donald Coggan came to receive her ministrations. Archbishop Robert Runcie sent a message read by the dean, affirming that 'your selfless ministry is an example to us all'. The London Chinese Christian community gave hundreds of the congregation a celebration lunch at St Martin-in-the-Fields. It was a rare morning of repentance and joy on behalf of the Church of England to a tiny woman who bore the trials of the pioneer with rare courage and a persuasive manner which fused intelligence and goodness. The day ended with rockets roaring over Trafalgar Square.

Florence Li was born in Hong Kong. Her doctor father had hoped for a son but called her Tim Oi, 'Much-Beloved Daughter'. At school Florence Nightingale was her heroine and she adopted her name. She began work as a teacher on the island of Ap Li Chau, opposite the fishing village of Aberdeen. Then she graduated from a four-year course in theology at Canton Union Theological College, intending to serve the Church as a lay worker. However, she was called to a ministry, and was ordained deacon to serve at Macau, still a free enclave as the Portuguese were not at war with the Japanese.

At Macau she ministered in English and Cantonese, and after the Japanese captured Hong Kong her congregation included hundreds of refugees who had left positions of responsibility in Hong Kong. Bishop Mok gave her permission to celebrate Holy Communion. She was also, like another Edith Cavell, caught up in the care of the wounded and the dying. News of her courage and the plight of the refugees reached R. O. Hall, Bishop of Hong Kong, who had managed to escape the Japanese army. He called Li to undertake a dangerous week-long journey through the Japanese lines to Xing Xing, where they spent several days in prayer and questioning. They then went, with other church members, to the church at Zhaoqing where he ordained her priest: the first woman to be a priest in the Anglican Communion.

After the war, Bishop Hall was censured and Li was told that, if she continued to work as a priest, the bishop would be compelled to resign. She wrote to Bishop Hall, 'I am a very tiny person, a mere worm', but she did not resign her orders, which she considered to be permanent, a gift from God which could not be erased. However, she ceased for many years to function officially as a priest, though she continued to work in places of need and sometimes of danger. During the Cultural Revolution she worked on a chicken farm sharing the privations of the people. In her own words, 'The waves have gone over us, but it was the Lord who brought the safety to the crest . . . Our belief is from our heart, so it does not matter when we go through the valley of the shadow of death.'

The end of the revolution led to her being called out once more as a priest to the fragile community of Christians beginning to form again in China. Before long, at Guangzhou, she was ministering to a congregation of a thousand. She finally retired to join other members of her family in Canada, but remained concerned about

England, whose language and culture she loved. To the end she supported the Movement for the Ordination of Women with prayer, generosity and the example of unobtrusive courage.

Christian Howard

Christian Howard was an outstanding lay leader in the Church of England. Her speaking, writing and personal example led many to think again about the traditional exclusion of women from the three-fold ministry.

She realized more quickly than many bishops and clergy that women had gifts to offer the Church which should be accepted for the sake of the Gospel and not rejected on anti-feminist grounds. Small, with brilliant blue eyes and a patrician tone of voice, she was an effective public speaker and on transatlantic lecture tours her humour captivated her audiences.

Christian Howard was born in 1916 at Castle Howard, the eldest of the five children of the Hon. Geoffrey and Christian Howard. Her father was an MP in Asquith's government, and her grandmother a prominent worker for women's suffrage. As a child, asked what she would like as a tenth birthday present, she said, 'a cricket match in the Castle Howard grounds'.

She was educated at home, at Folkestone, and at finishing schools in France and Italy. She gained a Lambeth Diploma in Theology and for two years taught Divinity at Chichester High School. Howard returned to the Diocese of York after two brothers were killed in the Second World War. She served the Girl Guide movement as a divisional commissioner and also became an international representative. As Secretary of the York Diocesan Board of Women's Work, a post which she held until 1979, her influence was widely felt. Archbishop Donald Coggan made her a lay canon provincial. As an elected representative, first on the Church Assembly and then on the General Synod, she played an important part for 25 years in the decision-making of the Church of England. From her usual position at the back of the hall, she frequently made a decisive late intervention, speaking without notes. She was the first woman vice-moderator of the Faith and Order Committee of the World Council of Churches.

Howard knew that the long haul to women's ordination needed a thorough background of scholarly work. She was asked to research learned studies of the place of women within different cultures and the contemporary discussion within the Christian churches. She wrote three major reports on the ordination of women, published in 1972, 1978 and 1984 – nearly 300 pages in all. She explored the views on women of Demosthenes, Plato and Aristotle and was equally well informed about Roman, Jewish, New Testament, Patristic, canon law and post-Reformation attitudes. Her researches and quick mind helped to change opinion in the Church of England.

She was well aware of overseas developments in ministry, especially in Hong Kong and in the US, but as she put it, 'In England everything stops for tea.' Howard insisted that 'In asking the question "Can a woman be ordained to the priesthood?" we are dealing not with a woman's question but what is good for the Church.' Some felt this as dismissive of women's search for justice. However, Howard was anxious to remain alongside the radicals and keep different views in harness together. The Movement for the Ordination of Women, of which she was a founding vice-moderator, was encouraged in its maintenance of different approaches by the knowledge that Howard had invited a woman priest from overseas to celebrate in the private chapel of Castle Howard. In this she was convinced she was not overstepping canon law. She devoted her chief energies to synodical action, frequently saying, 'I am a political animal.'

As the years passed, younger women moved into positions of leadership. But at a worldwide gathering of 2,500 people in Canterbury Cathedral in 1986, Howard opened the Declarations of Peace from around the world, announcing in her strong and striking voice, 'I bring Peace from the Province of York'. As one journalist put it, 'It felt like the first Pentecost, as 16 countries brought greetings to their doddering old Mum, the C of E, as she continues dithering and asking herself "Shall I or shan't I?"' Howard's determination, humour and generosity helped to carry the Church through to the final decision on 11 November 1992, when the Synod, by a two-thirds majority, agreed to the ordination of women as priests.

She was made a DBE in 1986. In her long illness, she was visited at her home in Coneysthorpe by friends from many countries. In her last weeks in hospital her bedside wall was enlivened by a purple tea-towel declaring 'A Woman's Place is in the House of Bishops'.

Sister Hilary of Wantage

Hilary Markey was given the idea of joining a religious community by a teacher. At the end of her career she spent 25 years living in a tiny flat in Waterloo on 'detached service' from the Wantage Community, welcoming visitors to Westminster Abbey and St Paul's. Her learned and good-humoured faith enabled her to develop an extraordinary gift for making friends with tourists from around the world; a steady stream of visitors found her, sometimes in mufti, sometimes in the blue habit of the Anglican Community of St Mary the Virgin at Wantage.

She had a long career in her community's schools at Plymouth, Abingdon and St Mary's, Wantage, as well as a time as deputy head at their school in apartheid days at Johannesburg. In London her strong sense of justice, especially for women, led her to volunteer as a helper at Amnesty International, Crisis at Christmas and the Movement for the Ordination of Women.

Her training was unusual. In her teens she used to travel on Saturdays by workman's bus at 6 a.m. from Burnley to the Sheffield library. She also contacted Alan Ecclestone to ask if she could come to his parish meeting and talk to him about the thinking of Bishop Leslie Hunter. After the Sheffield blitz in the bitter cold, with the windows blown out, she still worked at the university and also at Parson Cross, allegedly the largest parish in England. She also used opportunities to read music at Birmingham and theology at Oxford with David Jenkins, afterwards Bishop of Durham. She made her learning useful at Westminster Abbey for the monument to modern martyrs over the west door.

She valued modern and radical theologians – especially David Jenkins and Karl Rahner – and collected simplified ancient and modern creeds. She hoped the Free Churches and Roman Catholics would be welcomed in cathedrals and that the charging of visitors would be abandoned. She liked to quote 'God is all' and 'Religion is a plural thing', rejoicing especially on Trinity Sunday 2004 at St Paul's when the precentor, Canon Lucy Winkett, assisted by two other women priests, celebrated the main eucharist at the nave altar. She was always available to listen with a smiling face to the spiritual and human needs of others.

Sister Hilary's most thorough thought on Anglican spirituality was in her 1988 Sion College lecture on John Donne, who always inspired her. She liked quoting his words to describe the Bible, which he said was 'like a great wide sea in which a lamb may wade and an elephant swim'. She was conscious of humanity's various approaches to God and the many types of religious experience and tradition of the thousands from around the world who came as tourists to Westminster Abbey and St Paul's.

Donne knew that we must 'live with contraries'. Hilary connected this with John Keats's notion of 'negative capability' ('when man is capable of being in uncertainties, Mysteries, doubts without any irritable reaching after fact and reason'). For Hilary, herself a theologian, it reminded her of refugees on the frontiers – Paul Tillich, a refugee living with shaken foundations, or Jürgen Moltmann, a German prisoner in England, sure he was called to believe. So in Hilary's eyes, Donne's most famous words were to be true of us all:

> No man is an island, intire of itself. Everyman is a piece of the continent, a part of the maine; any man's death diminishes me, because I am involved in Mankind; and therefore never send to know for whom the bell tolls; it tolls for thee.

For Hilary 'the paw of friendship' was God's means of snatching us through our visits to churches or cathedrals or use of prayer books. God is a being of prayerfulness and passion and warm empathy, seeking to absorb pain and darkness, sharing a sense of fun and not taking self too seriously, especially with younger people. As Donne wrote:

> I cannot plead innocency of life, especially in my youth . . . I know
> He looks upon me now . . . as I am in my Saviour . . . I am full of
> inexpressible joy and shall dye in peace.

Hilary imagined that a twentieth-century Donne might have
been among those idealist poets who went off to the Spanish Civil
War or worked in the Third World or joined with the 1986 London
ecumenical expedition who travelled to Nicaragua, El Salvador and
Guatemala, where we in the Western churches worked together for
the freedom of the Central American Christians. Donne was an
activist. Perhaps his ordination on St Paul's Day, 25 June 1625, was
in order to obey the king and take part in the religious develop-
ment of the early Stuart period. Some of his greatest religious poems
were written in those years: 'At the round earth's imagined corners',
'Death be not proud', 'Batter my heart, three-personed God'.

Donne was also the era's greatest preacher. Again and again he
urged the virtue of constancy:

> He is a good Christian who can ride out a storm, that by industry,
> as long as he can, and by patience when he can do no more, over-
> rides a storm, and does not forsake his ship for it; that is not
> scandalized with that state, nor that church of which he is a
> member, for those abuses that are in it. It is well for us if though
> we be put to take in our sails, and to take down our masts, yet we
> can hull it out, that is if in storms of contradiction, of perse-
> cution by the Church or State . . . yet be able to subsist and swim
> above water and reserve itself for God's former glory, after the storm
> is past.

The Wantage Community composed intercessions for Hilary's
Requiem on 26 June 2007 of unusual beauty, thanking God for her
hidden qualities, for seeking to absorb the pain, darkness and confusion of those who felt marginalized, her knowledge and love of
the aesthetic world and the sense of interior beauty that St Paul
invoked in her. They said:

> We thank you for her strong commitment to justice, particularly on
> behalf of women in the Church. We pray for all who are drawn to
> maverick paths to express their inner truth.

Sister Hilary was widely influential and was elected to the General
Synod to represent the Anglican religious orders in the southern

province. After retiring from her tiny flat in a Church Commissioners' block at Waterloo she was welcomed back to the Community at Wantage, where visitors sought her out still, sharing her own quiet wisdom and smiling faith. *The Whispering Gallery* said:

> Her sense of fun, prayerfulness, humility, wit and intelligence will be missed by all that had the privilege of knowing her. Particularly the Virgers who always knew they could enlist her for a pastoral session or to give a specialist talk to a school group. We miss her at our morning coffee. (Michael Page)

Canon Ed Newell, preaching in St Paul's, said of Sister Hilary:

> For each of us, there will be special people who've helped us on our journey of faith.
>
> Last week, one person who's been an inspiration to many – and perhaps some of us here – died after a long and remarkable life. For many years, Sister Hilary Markey had a ministry both here in St Paul's and at Westminster Abbey.
>
> In that time she helped and encouraged many people in the faith, both those who worked and worshipped regularly, and visitors and pilgrims passing through.
>
> As her obituary in *The Times* reminds us, one of Sister Hilary's legacies is the set of statues of twentieth-century martyrs on the west front of Westminster Abbey. It was her research that helped determine which modern-day saints should be commemorated in this way.
>
> But her more important legacy is much less tangible – it's the influence that this remarkable woman of faith had on others.
>
> We must treasure such people, and give thanks to God for them, for we are who we are because of what they have given us.

At her funeral at Wantage, the following prayer was said:

> We thank you for Hilary's hidden qualities of seeking to absorb pain, darkness and confusion in those who felt marginalized.
>
> We thank you for her sense of fun, especially with younger people, and her wanting life or self not to be taken too seriously.
>
> We give thanks for her reaching out to the needs and searching of tourists, pilgrims, street-dwellers, staff and clergy in her 23 years of pastoral ministry at St Paul's Cathedral and her 12 years at Westminster Abbey.

We praise you for her seeking unobtrusively to affirm your presence in those whom she encountered.

Let us bless the Lord.

God of playfulness and passion:

We thank you for Hilary's knowledge and love of the aesthetic world, of musical form, of artistic image and architectural symmetry, and especially for the sense of interior beauty that St Paul's evoked in her.

We thank you for her strong commitment to justice, particularly on behalf of women in the Church and for her deep caring about the needs and suffering of those impoverished and oppressed.

She was iaid in a flower-decorated grave.

Building bridges from the City

The 1985 Church of England report, *Faith in the City*, drew attention to the plight of our inner cities and the contrast between life in comfortable Britain and the deprived areas. The attempt made to rubbish the report as Marxist was less than whole-hearted and quite wrong-headed.

It is comforting for battered bishops and lay churchpeople concerned with those who are poor, disadvantaged and feel excluded from the mainstream of our national life that the government is giving time this autumn to planning urban regeneration as a priority.

The Church is taking many initiatives to meet the spiritual and material needs of the deprived. In January 1986, a group of members of City institutions, convened by myself, as Dean of St Paul's, under the chairmanship of Sir Richard O'Brien, began considering how the City, the financial dynamo of the country, can respond.

A seconded manager services the group; discussions in the deanery and the Chapter House at St Paul's culminated last January at the

Bank of England, when the governor and the Archbishop of Canterbury addressed the problem.

Dr Runcie appealed for partnership at all levels, for the spirit of 'can do', which he found in the City of London, and which he sensed could also be evoked in the urban priority areas. He pleaded for more questions to be asked about the long-term implications of City decisions.

The archbishop followed up his speech with a letter to a number of chairmen of leading City companies posing two questions: whether non-commercial initiatives should be left to the government and private citizens, and what greater responsibility a company could accept towards people in the urban priority areas.

He admitted that for too long 'the church corporately has not seriously engaged with the complex and difficult realities of those trying to succeed in the competitive world of commerce and industry'.

But he pointed out that the churches in the United Kingdom consist of some seven million individuals, many of whom work in finance. They want to know how the Church and the private sector can work together to deal with the polarization which has developed in our society. Many of the recipients have put these questions to their boards and replied to the archbishop's questions.

Members of the St Paul's group went to Sheffield and to the Midlands to meet industrialists, local government leaders and the unemployed. Commenting on the Lower Don Valley at Sheffield, an accountant remarked: 'It resembles a great city after the blitz. Vast areas have been razed to the ground. A few of the buildings stand like huge empty cathedrals, their contents sold or scrapped, their work force gone.' He commented on the depression caused by unemployment, and by long hours of waiting in DHSS offices, sometimes being treated as a scrounger when you would like nothing better than to find a proper job once more.

Faith in the City is changing the Church's agenda. An urban fund is being created to enable projects of many kinds – church community centres, job creation schemes involving churches in inner-city areas – to be financed. The Archbishops of Canterbury and York wrote to all the clergy, asking them to prepare for the campaign, which was designed to offer hope in the deprived areas, and which was launched in April 1988, in an effort to raise £18 million.

This concern in the City strengthens commitment to worship, belief and prayer. Modern Christians wish the church to come out of the stained-glass-window buildings into the world, and deepen their discipleship.

Contemporary Christians are challenged by the Parable of the Talents. Like the wicked servant, we have hidden the extraordinary powers of science and technology so that our amazing competence does not go to meet the needs of the alienated and the poor: so often we use science to make rich groups and wealthy countries richer.

Faith in the City asked whether and how our financial institutions can have a corporate conscience about the deprived areas, how caring can shape the policy of companies, and how competition can be combined with compassion and concern for the whole of our society. These questions are implicit in ethical investment.

Many companies, but far from the majority, have a tradition of helping particular areas. East End Compact was launched by the Prince of Wales, drawing on the resources of the Inner London Education Authority and a number of City-based companies.

But there is still too great a gulf between the City and its neighbour, the East End; between Brick Lane and the canyons of Mammon in the City.

Thousands suffer from the great changes in our Western economy. The Gospels still address us: 'I was hungry and you gave me no food. I was thirsty and you gave me no drink. I was a stranger and you did not welcome me.' How can either the Church or the City stand before this judgement if they do not address these fundamental human needs?

Constructive disagreement

In an age of terrorism we pay attention to religious quarrels. The Precentor of St Paul's, Canon Lucy Winkett, has suggested that a sea change in the churches could take place as a result of women's ordination – 'if we could learn to disagree well'.

Cathedrals have, in fact, often been the scene of disagreement. Can they be laboratories of the spirit, where religious quarrels are addressed by teams, lay and ordained, working, thinking, sharing and suffering together?

A former MP for the Cities of London and Westminster, a faithful friend of St Paul's, recently sent me a copy of the 1649 Act of the Commons of England, which abolished deans and chapters. Trustees were to collect their revenues after 'a speedy exact and particular survey ... for the Army in England ... the war in Ireland ... and continuing at sea a stronger Navy than usual'. This record of a gigantic row scarcely rivals Hagia Sophia becoming a mosque and Notre Dame a temple of reason, but it is significant in the religious history of England.

The 11-year liquidation of cathedrals was resisted in Norwich by a devout shepherd from Earlham. He came to live in the cathedral candle room. Dean and chapter, choir and congregation had vanished, but by day he wandered the city's streets proclaiming 'Good cheer' and prophesying that king and bishop and cathedral would return.

They used to put him in the Bridewell prison. By night he slept in the deserted cathedral, the wind whistling through the smashed windows, with a piece of stone debris which he called his Jacob's ladder as his pillow. He was buried with his stone in the cloister. Soldiers left a bullet in the tomb of Bishop Goldwell, but the long witness of this powerless, homeless, believing shepherd was remembered.

The strife, political, social and religious, which led to the execution both of the king and of the Archbishop of Canterbury, was partly fuelled by theological and clerical authoritarianism. It is endemic in all religious priesthoods. Even in the nineteenth century all the bishops voted against Catholic Emancipation and against the Reform Bill – except for the bishops of Chichester and Norwich.

In our times, however, Pope John XXIII, Archbishop William Temple, Martin Luther King, Desmond Tutu and Dietrich Bonhoeffer have practised and preached ecumenism. Often it has been in cathedrals where their most courageous witness was made – as at Canterbury, when John Paul II and Robert Runcie prayed together.

Elsewhere black-led churches have assembled at St Paul's and German/British congregations have gathered at Coventry. Archbishop Oscar Romero's catafalque in San Salvador Cathedral draws hundreds daily to remember his martyrdom for social justice.

There are limitations, however, to cathedrals as centres of eirenic and rational agreement. Canon Winkett has, like many women priests, experienced opposition. It is good news that two woman theologians have been appointed at the Vatican and that the Church of Scotland this year has its first woman moderator.

Some, nevertheless, find this a difficult question to face. The possibility of women bishops in England is much reduced by the Act of Synod – an embarrassing fact for a Church pleading that male Anglican bishops should remain in a reformed House of Lords. Christian exclusiveness is not a wise symbol for a world where religious fundamentalism is dangerous.

Cathedrals have been home to many reconcilers and laboratories for many experiments. Dean Dammers of Bristol travelled to Monte Cassino to take services for Poles, Italians, Britons and Germans with whom he had once served in the bloody battles for that hill. The minister of the Edinburgh High Kirk, Gilleasbuig Macmillan, has shown that the Presbyterian Church of Scotland can have an episcopal colleague. Edward Patey of Liverpool fostered relationships between his cathedral and the Roman Catholic cathedral at the other end of Hope Street.

No doubt the new generation of women deans, canons and archdeacons will follow these peacemaking pioneers. The churches need to learn to disagree well, whether on the rights of women, homosexuality or liturgy. Great buildings used for worship and caring by generation after generation can give a sense of proportion to contemporary disputations.

Can cathedrals share the sorrows and joys of their cities?

Critics of cathedrals have sometimes compared them to fully rigged, four-masted ships imprisoned in bottles, needing someone to break the bottle, free the ship and allow it to be tossed by the waves and storms of life. *St Paul's* (Yale University Press), the magnificent volume commemorating the 1,400th anniversary of the founding of St Paul's, tells a story of repeated alienation between cathedral and society, followed by rebuilding, reform and revitalization of architecture, music, forms of worship and pastoral and educational concern. St Paul's has been burnt down four times but generations have loved it and rebuilt it – for the good of London. Forty-two scholars contribute essays to the book. It is lavishly illustrated with a cover taken from a detail of Canaletto's *Thames on Lord Mayor's Day*. Pictures range from those of the old medieval building, with its famous spire from which acrobats used to perform, to a picture of Henry Moore in a wheelchair looking at his *Mother and Child*. He said, with a twinkle, 'I am a regular churchman. I go to Matins on Christmas Day.'

The humanist dean John Colet (1467–1519) preached for the clergy to reform, but trusted his reorganized St Paul's School to the laity in the form of the Mercers' Company. St Paul's itself was to suffer from clerical intolerance. Three of its staff were burnt for being Protestants, and Bishop Bonner condemned 113 heretics mainly in St Paul's Consistory Court. Jesuits perished in St Paul's churchyard but recently one from Central America assisted at Holy Communion. Intolerant religion was experienced by John Donne (Dean 1621–31) whose family was related to the martyr Sir Thomas More. Progress towards toleration was slow and St Paul's was in danger of becoming a police station for enforcing uniformity. It was a happy chance that when reform came Canon Sydney Smith was in the pulpit of St Paul's to plead for Catholic emancipation as well as a peaceful foreign policy. The cathedral's preachers Colet, Donne and Smith tackled crucial issues in the religious life of Britain and Europe. St Paul's also provided a national mausoleum for Nelson and Wellington. As John Donne said: 'Religion is a plural thing.'

In the past century those who wanted the cathedral to engage with unemployment, war, nationalism and the treatment of women had their struggles. Canon Dick Sheppard, who had made St Martin-in-the-Fields a lively centre of compassion, was not even allowed to introduce a Christmas tree. (He persuaded the king to send one from Sandringham and his cautious colleagues did not have the nerve to return it to Norfolk.) Canon John Collins used the cellar of 2 Amen

Court to run International Defence and Aid, as it was secure from the attentions of the South African police. He also invited Muslims to hold a service in the crypt, and the Berlin Philharmonic Orchestra to play under the dome soon after the end of the war.

The Movement for the Ordination of Women was nurtured in Amen Court and St Paul's now has three women priests. In both 1918 and 1945 crowds assembled and demanded extra services to thank God for peace.

Hidden away in this history are two lay names of those who have reshaped English cathedrals for the twenty-first century – Sir Richard O'Brien, chairman of the *Faith in the City* report, and Elspeth Howe, chairman of the Commission on Cathedrals. Both were members of the cathedral's Court of Advisers, volunteers who gave much wisdom to the cathedral's duties and opportunities. Now all major decisions in all cathedrals on worship, finance and policy involve lay women and men. The old clerical monopoly of power is gone. At St Paul's the concern to find a way to share the gospel is represented by the dialogues in the autumn of 2004 in which the Archbishop of Canterbury, Dr Rowan Williams, and other thinkers and statesmen discussed 'the worlds in which we live'. This cathedral ship is making a voyage which matters for the future, and continues to provide London with a historic setting for reflection, prayer and thanksgiving.

The Church's one foundation

When Bishop Henry McAdoo of the Church of Ireland left his home in the old palace at Kilkenny, the road to the station for his train to Dublin was lined with cheering men and women, most of them Roman Catholic. This Irish-speaking bishop, who has died aged 81, was respected by the community; and he was an expert fly-fisher, always willing to share a pipe.

Though the Church of Ireland, of which he was bishop, was a minority in the town, he was looked upon with affection by the community, which regretted his departure to become archbishop. The community felt one of their own was leaving.

Henry Robert McAdoo was educated at Cork Grammar School and Mountjoy School in Dublin. He was ordained in 1939 and, while serving in various parishes, became a prolific author. He was recognized, with Archbishop George Sims, as one of the leading scholars of his church. He read widely the Anglican Caroline Divines, especially Jeremy Taylor, the seventeenth-century Anglican thinker who had been imprisoned before becoming an Irish bishop.

Like Taylor, McAdoo was tolerant, learned and devout, concerned with the real presence in the eucharist. McAdoo expounded Anglicanism as a disciplined way of sacramental devotion, free from ecclesiastical dictation. He saw in Anglicanism a form of Christianity which was enthused with liberality, while being both catholic and reformed.

His learning and temperament fitted him for the great task of his life – to become one of the chairmen of ARCIC, the Anglican–Roman Catholic International Commission, which worked from 1967 to 1981. Here, for the first time since the split 400 years ago, representative scholars authorized by their churches met over a prolonged period to talk in friendship, faith and trust. They concentrated on central issues: the sacraments, the ministry and authority. Their lengthy reports still lie on the tables of the churches. McAdoo believed the agreements would one day bridge the Reformation rift. A new language would enable the churches to express together the truths so dear to each of them.

McAdoo led these meetings over the years with a group of international scholars in London, Venice, Malta and Windsor. He developed great skill as co-chairman with the Roman Catholic bishop Alan Clark. He was confident that progress could be made and, aided by his scholarship, linguistic abilities and concentration, a language of convergence and ecumenical trust was found.

He knew the agenda so well that he could watch everyone's face and catch every nuance. He could be firm – almost a prince-bishop – able to silence even an American Jesuit or an Australian archbishop. Himself an old-fashioned Protestant high churchman, he understood the antagonisms.

Some of those round the table feared that the eirenic statements might be seen, by hitmen, as treason to Rome and McAdoo might be in personal danger. Others greatly regretted the delays and hostility of the Vatican bureaucracy. Both McAdoo and Clark were rightly awarded the Cross of Canterbury.

With hindsight he felt Rome and the churches lost an opportunity. To his regret, fundamentalism was to grow within the institutions and there was less loyalty to the decisions of synods or bishops. In the mainstream churches, McAdoo lamented a reduction in the full-time ministry. The last of his books traced how tradition might have to be questioned to strengthen the ministry by the ordination of women.

McAdoo's status within Anglicanism, for which he modestly enthused, depended in part on the fact that he was not English. He was not appointed by the English Establishment. He could make fun of the sectarianism of both Evangelicals and Catholics within the Church of England. Asked on a media occasion whether the ARCIC agreement could help the Church of England he adopted a strong Irish brogue: 'You will not be asking me as an Irishman that.'

He and his wife Lesley were witty and warm-hearted, and their home was a place of *joie de vivre*. Irish culture delighted him and he was especially happy in Trinity College, Dublin. By being himself he was a focus of understanding. In his words:

Those who have worked at the coalface of Christian unity have soon discovered the paradox that the more truly they express, in love, their own tradition the better they are able to understand in depth and to value the other tradition, with which they are in dialogue. Confrontational attitudes dissolve.

McAdoo was a great reconciler, recognized as a leader of sterling worth.

Alan Ecclestone

Shortly after the bombing of Hiroshima a protest procession wound its way through the blitzed East End streets of Sheffield. It was led by Alan Ecclestone with the members of the Church of Holy Trinity, Darnall – one of the courageous and prophetic acts which marked his 27 years as vicar.

Ecclestone was the most challenging and radical of all the Church's parish priests, a George Herbert of the inner city; like Herbert he was catholic in his sacramentalism and committed to the welfare of people in his parish whether they went to church or not, and again like Herbert a scholar and writer. He summed up his spirituality in a contemporary classic on prayer, *Yes to Prayer* (1975, awarded the Collins Religious Book prize). After his retirement to Gosforth he won more admirers with his *Staircase for Silence* (1977, showing his love for Charles Péguy), his *Night Sky of the Lord* (1980, on the churches' need to heed the Jewish experience) and *Scaffolding for the Spirit* (1987, insights into St John's Gospel).

Ecclestone was the son of a Stoke-on-Trent pottery painter. His mother, more radical than his father, used to put up a 'Home Rule' for Ireland poster in their window but removed it before father returned from work. Scholarships gained Alan Firsts in History and English at Cambridge and a lectureship in English at Durham. The sight of unemployed miners and the teaching of the Catholic Crusade in the Church of England were powerful counter-influences to a university career, especially the radical priests Jim Wilson, of Burslem, and Conrad Noel, of Thaxted, who intertwined the Red Flag and the Cross of St George for their demonstrations. Ecclestone deserted senior common room talk for a lifelong love affair with the Workers' Educational Association (WEA) and was trained for the church at Wells and ordained by Dr Henry Herbert Williams, the philosopher-bishop of Carlisle. He married Delia Abraham, who shared his campaigning determination – her 'Amens' loudly spoken at the end of prayers seemed always admonitions to the Almighty.

Alan Ecclestone's first living was at Frizington, in Cumberland, where three-quarters of the men were unemployed miners – in his words, 'a marvellous heart-rending place. TB was rife and the poverty was appalling. But they were wonderful people to be with.'

In 1942 he joined Bishop Leslie Hunter's team in Sheffield and spent the next 27 years as vicar of Darnall. He and Delia were convinced that the Church needed major changes. Though he admired Hunter as 'the greatest bishop I have ever known' and represented the diocese in the Church Assembly and Convocation, these were not his scene; he devoted himself to the ideal of transforming the Church into a network of living communities, able to change 'the devilish society in which we live into something nearer the Kingdom of God'.

His ministry in Sheffield developed the strategy of the parish community and the parish meeting as basic weekly events in which the congregation learned to experience the discipline and exhilaration of becoming a close-knit community of friends with a common life-purpose and plan of action. He lost a few parishioners to this demanding regime but won many more both in the parish and outside. At a parish meeting, sitting in his cassock, alert, laughing, on the floor of the stone-flag kitchen with 30 or 40 parishioners of all ages slowly becoming articulate, he was a brilliant animator and summarizer. Hints were heard: Delia agreed to stop selling copies of the *Daily Worker* before the service (she sold them afterwards outside). Popular Catholicism in the Church of England was at its lively best. A form of church life increasingly influential in other parishes was slowly evolved and Darnall vicarage became a place of pilgrimage as Ecclestone sought to reintegrate the Church and the working community. Services were full of light, processions, and enjoyable symbolism. He used to say, 'Marrying the children whose parents you have married is a wonderful thing.'

He was also a leader of the Christian–Marxist dialogue in the post-war years. He attended the left-wing peace conferences at Paris and Warsaw and stood six times unsuccessfully as a Communist councillor for solidly Labour Sheffield. He welcomed the revolution in China and was happy that one of his sons went to work there. When accused of naivety he would quote Josef Hromadka, the wartime Czech Christian leader, that one must go with the people and share their centuries-old struggle.

In the Cold War years he was isolated by his membership of the Communist Party. The party, Ecclestone said, was as bemused to have a priest for a member as the parish was to have a Communist as their priest. In later years he did not support the party but pleaded for a sharing of property and a renunciation of the power structures:

'God has renounced power and approaches us only with love.' His personal way of life and humour won him a hearing even when Stalinism and McCarthyism bedevilled understanding.

Prayer as the link between the divine and the human was at the heart of his faith. He used an imaginative 'communion for married couples' before and during Delia's long illness. In hospital they could be heard singing Compline quietly before he caught his bus home.

In 1987 his Good Friday Three Hours' Devotion at St Paul's was a compelling reassertion of the cross as the scene of the struggle for justice. Supported by his loyal and talented family he continued to the end, generously available for conferences, retreats and a constant succession of friends who travelled to Cumberland to walk and talk with him. Wherever he was, he was loved and respected. His writings and letters were treasured, and his own discipleship was convincingly encouraging to the end of a long life.

Edward Carpenter

Edward Carpenter was a highly original Dean of Westminster who enabled Westminster Abbey to become a shrine welcoming a great variety of good causes. After 20 years as a learned, hard-working and unpushy north London parson he was 'discovered' by Clement Attlee and spent 35 years at the abbey, eventually becoming Dean from 1974 to 1986. He and his much respected wife, Lilian, will go down in the history of Westminster for being so accessible, friendly and prepared to listen.

Carpenter was a thorough Londoner, educated at Strodes School, Egham, and King's College in the Strand. As a historian he published major episcopal biographies as well as being a popular speaker and lecturer. His personal routine included watching Chelsea Football Club, of which he was an enthusiastic supporter, working through the night on his historical researches and spending time by day on the abbey floor, concerned to be with visitors and staff.

Though naturally shy and short-sighted he was always prepared to make new friends and consider new points of view. He injected a happy vagueness into ceremonial occasions which might otherwise have been boring or pretentious and (like the Queen Mother) managed to greet others without impropriety in church processions.

He commended the Christian faith to thoughtful people, where more media-conscious or mission-driven leaders might be offputting. He understood the objections. He is remembered with affectionate esteem by lay people of all churches, and by humanists and members of other faiths, including Jews, Buddhists, Hindus, Muslims and Baha'is.

Though himself always personally committed, he defended the Commonwealth ceremony at the abbey where the world's religions expressed their beliefs together. His scholarly impartiality in his historical publications is shown in his gentle treatment of Bishop Henry Compton, the last bishop to bear arms, and of the managerial Archbishop Geoffrey Fisher, who so opposed the Anglican–Methodist reunion proposals. No reader would guess that Carpenter himself was a pacifist, an ecumenist and a feminist.

However, he was a discreet but firm opponent of twentieth-century intolerance. When both Downing Street and Lambeth believed that a 'realistic' approach to South Africa required compromise, Carpenter would have none of it. When some rejected the ordination of women on the ground that it was unprecedented, Carpenter offered the abbey to celebrate the fortieth anniversary of the ordination of the Chinese pioneer priest Florence Li Tim Oi in 1984, eight years before the General Synod and Parliament removed the legal barriers in England. It was characteristic on that historic occasion that it was Carpenter who noticed that there were not enough chairs for the congregation and had more carried in.

He was prepared to face opposition even from scholarly archbishops whom he respected. He did not believe that Archbishop William Temple was radical enough in his attitudes to either capitalism or business sleaze. When Michael Ramsey refused to have anything to do with the World Congress of Faiths, Carpenter persisted, without success, in trying to persuade Ramsey to change his mind. Carpenter was committed to faith in the Trinity and in Christ but Ramsey felt this was put in doubt if all 'religions' were welcomed. Carpenter was more aware than Ramsey of the variety of spiritual searching in contemporary society.

'Management' was not one of Carpenter's priorities. He did not attend the Church Commissioners. He searched for and gave his mind to bodies where he saw imagination and concern for a happier human future. So he was an energetic member of the Modern Church-people's Union, the World Congress of Faiths, the Shelley Society, the Byron Society, the United Nations Association, the Council for Christians and Jews and the Council for the Welfare of Animals. His determination to help women's education was shown in his chairmanship of the Mary Buss Foundation, the North London Collegiate School, the Camden School for Girls and the St Anne's Society. The fact that occasionally he might arrive breathless by bicycle or have simultaneous appointments did not decrease the warmth of the welcome he received.

In his concern with worship in his parishes and at the abbey he was conscious of the man and woman in the street. He wanted worship to be accessible and urged brevity, time for silence, reflection and meditation – hence his love of the abbey's music. He liked the drive of Cranmer's succinct phrase 'whose service is perfect freedom'.

For him Christ's teaching reflected in lessons or sermon had the individual ring of spiritual genius about it. Slogans, pressures and hype were all out of place: as he remarked, 'There need be nothing dramatic about entering into the kingdom, for in some sense it is equivalent to a new birth, to be raised to the fullness of life, even when one is old.'

He felt happily serendipitous, his suspicions of codified morals reinforced, when he discovered in Barrow School chapel, before preaching there, a Prayer Book with the Table of Kindred and Affinity on the last page, on which, against the injunction that 'a man may not marry his grandmother', a schoolboy had written, 'Lord, have mercy upon us, and incline our hearts to keep this law.'

Though at the heart of the establishment, both ecclesiastic and political, Carpenter remained surprisingly unpompous and unexpected. He emphasized the freshness of the divine, which brings us into new situations in which each person's conscience may require a sacrificial decision. He had no fear of science and greatly admired the wisdom of those seventeenth-century ecclesiastics who threw their energies into the Royal Society. He pleaded for imaginative understanding of others and commended the children's prayer 'O God, make the nice people good; and the good people nice'.

It was unfortunate for the Church that Edward Carpenter was 64 before he became dean but he has left a legacy of tolerant, determined openness as a vital trait of twentieth-century Christianity. He and his wife gave themselves unstintingly to others and contributed a happy sparkle in their home at Westminster in their laughter and scholarship.

Kenneth Sansbury

Kenneth Sansbury was one of the ablest of English priests. He served the Church in a series of posts in different parts of the world during and after the shock waves of the Second World War and the break-up of the Empire, working with energy and common sense to strengthen the relationships which enabled the Anglican Communion to remain united despite major theological, political and social changes.

After a double First in Theology at Cambridge and a curacy in Dulwich, he went as a missionary to Japan, first in Numazu and next in Tokyo, where he was professor of the Central Theological College, serving a number of tiny churches as well as being chaplain to several British institutions, including the Embassy.

Sansbury's appreciation of Japanese culture remained with him all his life: he even looked a little Japanese thereafter. In his last days he was delighted with the news that a Japanese priest served weekly to welcome Japanese visitors in St Paul's and Westminster Abbey. He remained 'our beloved Sansbury' to many Japanese church leaders.

After Pearl Harbor he and his wife Etheldreda and their family were evacuated to Canada, where he enlisted as a chaplain in the Royal Canadian Air Force. Conscientious as ever, he was known as 'the chap with the English accent'. In 1943 he became Warden of

Lincoln Theological College, transforming that institution in order to welcome an influx of married service ordinands. He appointed an able staff, including John Yates, afterwards Bishop of Gloucester, Basil Moss, afterwards Provost of Birmingham, and John Fenton, the distinguished New Testament teacher. They continued the tradition inherited from Michael Ramsey and Eric Abbott of radical theology and Catholic devotion but transformed what Sansbury described as 'this awful monastic existence' into a community in which those who had been serving in the Forces throughout the world felt welcome and appreciated for their abilities. Etheldreda, a scholar in her own right, was a warm-hearted, intelligent friend to the servicemen and their wives. Sansbury gave excellent leadership, was quick at grasping the gist of an issue or a book, and able to assess the characters of those whom he was training with sure judgement.

After seven years at Lincoln Sansbury accepted the more demanding task of Warden of St Augustine's, Canterbury, an institution founded by Joshua Watson in 1846 to train missionaries. It was now hoped it might become a central college for the Anglican Communion. In practice clergy, often with their wives and families, came especially from Africa and India for varying periods for study, retraining and refreshment. Sansbury faced difficulties of staffing, finance, buildings, and drawing together the ultra-conservative and those who wanted change, those who came from wealthy Western backgrounds and those whose home churches were extremely poor.

This taxed all his diplomatic powers but he did not shirk the difficulties which would beset formerly colonial churches when their countries became independent. In the comparative calm of Canterbury he tried to warn the future leaders of their heavy responsibilities. Many years later a former St Augustine's student, working as a senior church leader in Africa, put the sad little sentence at the bottom of a Christmas card, 'You were wiser than I', in token of tensions foreseen by Sansbury but not by the student.

In 1961 he was consecrated as the last expatriate Bishop of Singapore and Malaya. Sansbury, now 56, braved tedious travelling in the tropics and taught and preached with his customary skill and energy. Perhaps Archbishop Geoffrey Fisher, often ultra-cautious, would have been wiser to have chosen a young non-European for this very rapidly developing Asian diocese. A cathedral service in Singapore might use seven different languages. Sansbury felt keenly the ecclesiastical and political divisions imposed by history, European traders, colonial powers and missionaries. Etheldreda was always acute in grasping subtleties of relationships and poured herself out in intelligent concern and hospitality, but after five years they were both glad to return to England.

In 1956 he succeeded Dr Kenneth Slack as General Secretary of the British Council of Churches, one of the few Anglicans to hold that post. It was a difficult inheritance, for Slack was a popular national figure, well known as an effective broadcaster. But Sansbury brought his own ecumenical experience at Evanston, New Delhi and Bossey at a time when hopes were high for reunion.

He was a loyal assistant of Archbishop Ramsey, went to Nigeria at his request as a mediator in the civil war – a dangerous flight – and supported the efforts to reconcile Anglicans and Methodists in England. He published first *Unity, Peace and Concord* (1967) and later *Combating Racism* (1975). His enthusiasm was endless but the introversion and traditionalism of some Anglican bishops and clergy, the false hopes raised by Vatican II, and the slide into a more consumerist and secular society alienated him. After the failure of the reunion schemes he gallantly kept the British Council of Churches alive as a body campaigning for reunion and radical Christianity.

Sansbury retired to Norwich in 1973, where he was an honoured member of the staff of the cathedral. He cared for those who lived in the Close, was warm-hearted in his pastoral work, punctilious in his concern to listen to lay opinion. His instinct to respect and appreciate other people's points of view grew even stronger with the years. He and Etheldreda were part of a web of relationships and friends in the UK and abroad which was a source of joy to them and to their adopted city.

Oliver Tomkins

Oliver Tomkins was an experienced British ecumenist. He served the Church of England as a vicar, the principal of a theological college and as a diocesan bishop, but he always remained a leader in the long process of bringing the Christian churches to understand each other. He was a student all his days, with remarkable powers of clarity and analysis.

Tomkins was not sentimental about ecumenism. He felt that if his contemporaries were to believe in God, and to trust the churches' claims about being communities of reconciliation, they had no option but to understand each other and to live in much greater peace and cooperation. Ecumenism was not an optional extra, a fad of some people in Rome or Geneva. It was a test of the churches' claim. He described the ecumenical movement as Balaam's ass, which showed churches who run away from each other into isolationism that they are faced with an angel with a drawn sword barring their retreat. To shirk reconciliation was to ignore a divine demand. Oliver Tomkins had a touch of genius in his ability to describe the beliefs and ways of life of different Christian communities to each other.

Tomkins's deep-set, smiling eyes seemed to be looking beyond the parochial Anglican scene, and his background prepared him for his special role. His father was a missionary at Hangchow, in China, where Oliver was born. Another relative was a Congregationalist martyr in the Pacific islands.

Tomkins was early influenced by the evangelical ecumenical leader Edward Woods (whose life he wrote, not uncritically, in 1957), but much more by his time on the staff of the Student Christian Movement (SCM) in the 1930s and later of the World Council of Churches (WCC), where he was Secretary of the Faith and Order Commission. His colleagues in the SCM and the WCC came from all the non-Roman churches and formed an inter-church ministerial group of great ability, including David Paton, William Greer, Davis McCaughey (later Governor of the State of Victoria), Philip Lee Woolf, Alan Richardson, Ronald Preston, David Say and, at Geneva, the great old man of the ecumenical movement, Dr Visser't Hooft. Annual conferences for students at Swanwick conference centre, in Derbyshire, kept him in touch with the views of the young, and his correspondence with the formidable headmasterly Archbishop Geoffrey Fisher shows how seriously he was taken by the leader of his own church.

Tomkins took part in setting up the World Council of Churches at Amsterdam in 1948, participated in the Lund Conference on Faith and Order in 1952, and was constantly on the move from country to country, meeting church leaders. He stressed, so far as he could to the governments of their countries, the need to allow the churches the freedom to share in the restoration of a fresh post-war world.

Oliver and his wife Ursula were summoned home by the Church of England, some of whose leaders felt that they were becoming detached from the English scene. He became Warden of Lincoln Theological College, and suffered considerable cultural shock. It was not only that England was so introverted – especially in its church life, as Archbishop Fisher led determinedly into the intricacies of canon law – but as contrasted with post-war Europe, so determined on reconstruction, the scene at Lincoln was difficult. The salary was small and the established habits of the college were in some ways monastic. Tomkins was extremely loyal to tradition, but he moved the college forward and he and Ursula enabled the wives to feel that they were valued members of the community. A Jesuit visitor at the college soon afterwards said that the ordinands' wives were making a greater personal sacrifice, not only than their husbands, but even than Jesuits training for the Society of Jesus.

Oliver's presence, with his world reputation, did much for a college which had already had a reputation for radical New Testament theology, and traditional Catholic worship. However, it was not an easy period and he was relieved when he was summoned in 1959 to the much more liberated task of being Bishop of Bristol.

Taking over Oliver's study (I succeeded him as Warden of Lincoln), I was surprised to find a drawer he had forgotten to clear – his nickname was 'Tidy Tomkins'. The drawer was full of street maps of the world's major cities – Tokyo, Paris, Amsterdam and New York among them. Underneath was quite a stock of gold coins. I rang up Bristol, enquiring how to get these valuables to him, and asked, 'Why the gold?' He replied, 'On ecumenical journeys, I always find, especially in Abyssinia, that gold is the most effective coinage.' His charm, determination, humour and sheer integrity got him through so many barriers; whether he was discussing European ecumenism with the Queen of the Netherlands, or visiting the centres of power in Addis Ababa, or part of a seminar with Reinhold Niebuhr and Paul Tillich in New York, he was always welcomed, recognized and trusted as a servant of world Christianity.

His 17 years as Bishop of Bristol enabled him to use his wide experience. Archbishop Fisher, who insisted on his appointment, rapidly took exception to many of his views, especially as Tomkins was uninterested in structures and hierarchical disputes – closer in sympathy to Michael Ramsey. Tomkins continued the intelligent ecumenism of his predecessor in Bristol, F. A. Cockin, and was one of those who pioneered local ecumenical experiments in parishes. He found opportunities for laity and clergy to grow together in understanding the call of the gospel. In 1964 Tomkins presided over the Nottingham Faith and Order Conference, which hoped for church reunion in England by Easter 1980. The virtual jilting at the altar which Anglicans administered to Methodists grieved him greatly. The trust shown in him by opposite wings of the church – both the Church Union under Fr Percy Coleman and the Evangelicals – in setting up Trinity College, Bristol, facilitated the work of the diocese, though he would have preferred fully ecumenical theological colleges.

He also won the trust of younger clergy and could be both a father in God and a Lord Bishop of the diocese to them. He could bless the ambiguity of marrying the divorced in church. He could both listen and lead, and took much trouble to support some government workers suddenly declared redundant. He encouraged the ministry of women: his last published booklet was on the need to ordain women to the priesthood. He would often celebrate in parishes at 8 a.m. on a Sunday to enable the clergy to take a holiday. He was a much respected bishop.

Generations of ordinands and their spouses, both in Lincoln and at Bristol, remember Ursula with great gratitude. She made it clear at Lincoln that wives were welcome – although they were not allowed to sing plainsong in chapel. At Bristol, to visit the Tomkinses' home was always a delight and strangely bonding, especially at ordination retreats. The newly arrived felt welcomed into a home which became theirs because they were working in the diocese. Oliver and Ursula were complementary hosts. One of the younger clergy said that the bishop seemed to inhabit a place that was both Olympian and down to earth, but you felt that Ursula always came down on the side of sanity, common sense and charity – demanding, compassionate, witty and surprising. Their 17 years at Bristol gave the diocese an unusual quality, as if it was a diocese in the world church.

Horace Dammers

The wartime Royal Artillery service of Horace Dammers, who died aged 83, was in North Africa and Italy with the Surrey and Sussex Yeomanry. It ended in 1944 when, severely wounded at the battle of Monte Cassino, he was stretchered down to a casualty dressing station.

There he found himself next to a wounded German pilot who noticed that Dammers was reading a Bible. The German said: 'I, too, read the Bible. I have found some comfort in it since my wife and two sons were killed in an RAF raid on Hamburg.' Dammers stretched out and touched the pilot's hand.

So began the ministry of peace and reconciliation of one of the most energetic, warm-hearted and radical clergy of his generation. It was recounted in his posthumously published autobiography *Thank you, Holy Spirit*. And he was to return to Monte Cassino to take part in services with Italians, Germans, Britons and Poles who had fought each other below the monastery.

Despite a damaged foot, Dammers's energy – he enjoyed sailing, squash and cricket – led him to minister where there was tension from war or from religious and cultural strife. He was one of those post-war ordinands in all the churches in Europe who hoped for an open Christendom devoted to the creation of a society aiming at unselfish compassion, turning away from church introspection and subverting what they saw as a dangerous culture of nationalistic capitalism.

Dammers was born in Great Yarmouth and given by his father a love of sailing and of Norfolk and its unofficial motto 'Do Different'. After Malvern College, Pembroke College, Cambridge, war service and Westcott House, Cambridge – where he married Brenda – in 1948 he was given a Lancashire curacy. After three years at the first ecumenical theological college, Queen's College, Birmingham, Horace and Brenda accepted a posting in South India, in 1953. He became chaplain and lecturer at St John's College, Palayamkottai, where at last Anglicans and Free Church ministers could work together.

In 1957 he became examining chaplain to Dr Leslie Hunter, the prophetic Bishop of Sheffield. As vicar of Millhouses he followed the ecumenist Dr Oliver Tomkins. In 1965 he was appointed canon and Director of Studies at the rebuilt Coventry Cathedral. Here he worked out the Common Discipline of the Community, a guide to a provision of time for prayer, study, work, family life, relaxation, worship and personal growth.

His years at Bristol Cathedral (1973–87) were creative. The importance of the cathedral to Bristol was evidenced by the huge number of services it hosted. Dammers's friendliness enabled these occasions to be more than formal. Civic, academic, legal, school and minority communities were all welcomed. He created a peace chapel used for Amnesty vigils and anti-apartheid prayers. Student volunteers worked in the crypt and there were occasions for Missions to Seamen and for the Life Style movement – which he had founded in 1972 – and its 'Live simply that others may simply live'. Some criticized the demanding range of welcome as bringing politics into religion, but many more were influenced in their search for a life of magnanimity and integrity.

One of Dammers's colleagues remarked: 'We talk; the Dean does.' He packed the cathedral with Roman Catholics saying Mass. At interfaith services the building resonated with the sound of 'Om'. Members of the Jewish faith and Asian minorities were among his friends.

The Anglican and Catholic choirs together visited Calcutta and sang to Mother Teresa's patients. His musical ability and natural approachableness won hearts wherever he went. In the cathedral, links with Monte Cassino, Bordeaux and Hanover were maintained. Dammers also had time for other cathedrals. He was careful that at Bristol the congregation was consulted and that decisions were taken by consensus, not by authority.

Critical of inherited privilege, he once controversially resigned the chairmanship of the governors of a cathedral school. He gave his time and his pen to many causes: the Friends of Reunion, One for Christian Renewal, the Ex-Services Campaign for Nuclear Disarmament, the campaign on landmines, the Corrymeela venture in Northern Ireland, efforts to care for the older generation and Cathedral Camps.

In retirement Dammers and his wife welcomed visitors to their home in Shirehampton and their clifftop cottage in north Norfolk. His wisdom, humour and faith hinted at the life of a twentieth-century St Francis.

Jim Bishop

Jim Bishop was an Anglican pastor and bishop whose integrity, conviction and personal friendliness were greatly valued by the communities he served, especially the Diocese of Bristol, the parish of St George's, Camberwell, and the village of Cley next the Sea. Tall, white-haired, grave but friendly, he avoided all forms of publicity. In his 21 years of a very active retirement in Norfolk he quietly encouraged religious renewal – in particular the Focolare and Julian Movements, and the Movement for the Ordination of Women. To the end of a long life he was trusted, consulted and welcomed.

Clifford Leofric Purdy Bishop (to give his never-used Christian names) was born in 1908, the son and grandson of Rectors of Cley. His father died when he was very young, and he was too shy to enjoy his time at St John's, Leatherhead and Christ's, Cambridge, but found himself when working in challenging inner-city parishes. He had trained at Lincoln Theological College, where Michael Ramsey, later to be Archbishop, was Sub-Warden. Bishop shared Ramsey's non-authoritarian catholicism, liberal and scholarly, pastoral and compassionate, inspired especially by the eucharist and the practice of meditation. Like Ramsey, he could be severe under his gentle manner; like Ramsey too, he was prepared to take risks in the hope of the reunion of Christians.

After curacies in Stoke Newington and Middlesbrough (with Fr Jonathan Graham, later Superior of Mirfield) Bishop spent creative war years at St George's, Camberwell, which was also the Trinity College Mission. He formed a team of men and women which included many outstanding pastors. Among the men were Howell Witt, later a bishop in Australia, Timothy Stanton, afterwards imprisoned in South Africa in the apartheid struggle and mentor of Desmond Tutu, and Jack Churchill, later Dean of Carlisle. With the sisters and women workers a life of discipline, humour and initiative bubbled at the clergy house.

Bishop encouraged schools, social workers and the Church to cooperate, especially in giving new opportunities to young people in Camberwell, whether through academic coaching or through group holidays. He liked his colleagues to remain unmarried for some years. This occasional source of difficulty was resolved in 1949 when his own marriage to Ivy Adams gave him a home and family which was to undergird his life.

After an interlude as Rector of Blakeney, where he shared the sufferings of north Norfolk during the great flood of 1953, he returned to the inner city – Bishopwearmouth, the parish church of Sunderland. Here he was less happy and felt out of sympathy with the traditions of that church. His real stature was revealed in his new work as Suffragan Bishop of Malmesbury in the diocese of Bristol.

His years at Bristol (1962–73), where he reinforced Bishop Oliver Tomkins's different gifts, won him lifelong friends among both clergy and lay people, who found him wise, approachable, discreet and inspiring. With Ivy, he re-created the laughter and homeliness of the life at Camberwell. On reaching the age of 65, Bishop said modestly, 'I have run out of ideas', and resigned. His self-assessment was far from true and his departure was greatly regretted.

Returning to Cley, he was in a village where he and Ivy and their family were already at home. After all, some of the older residents had seen him as a small child in his bath. His occasional sermons were models in their depth and simplicity, and the Communion services in his own home, attended by Free Church and Roman Catholic people as well as by those on the margins of the Church, struck a prophetic note. In his final illness, he confirmed a 12-year-old grandson and then insisted that the boy should bless him. It was characteristic of a distinguished and self-giving ministry which had spanned the generations.

Stanley Booth-Clibborn

Stanley Booth-Clibborn – Bishop of Manchester from 1979 to 1992 – was a controversial and energetic bishop of the Thatcher years.

His diocese had the largest group of run-down Urban Priority Area parishes and this impelled him to constant public pleas for a social order which would redress the balance in favour of the marginalized. In 1991 he published *Taxes: Burden or Blessing?*, which urged 'a radical change in our attitudes towards what we do in common and how we pay for it'. He was an Anglican rarity – a bishop who was known to belong to the Labour Party – whether speaking in a downtown pulpit in Salford or in the House of Lords.

This least pontifical of bishops came from the Booth family, which had founded the Salvation Army, and he married Anne Forrester, member of a family distinguished for service in the Church of Scotland. Again he was unusual among Anglican bishops in feeling at home in radical and Reformed circles, both political and ecclesiastical.

But he was not a 'party man'. He was scrupulous in his policy of appointing conservatives and Catholics to posts in his diocese. His natural sympathies were with radical causes: inner-city parishes, support for the developing world, and the ordination of women as priests. Through his wife Anne, a deputy chairman of Christian Aid, he had wide international contacts.

Brisk, hard-working, likeable, Booth-Clibborn was born in London, educated at Highgate School, and then spent five years' commissioned service in the Royal Artillery, including two years in India. At Oriel College, Oxford, many of his friends were destined for politics but he decided to offer himself for ordination. After four years in east-end parishes in Sheffield he served in Kenya for 11 years in ecumenical posts.

He was appointed Editor-in-Chief of East African Venture Newspapers, a project which was designed to draw together the churches and the developing African leadership. I once heard him speaking in a shop-front church in Nairobi, challenging his African congregation to prepare for political struggles when independence came. When a worshipper rebuked him by claiming that this was politics, not religion, he insisted that God was calling the congregation to be responsible for their own nation, adding, 'Politics is not a dirty business Africans can leave to the British.' He also advocated the freeing of Jomo Kenyatta from prison, basing this on his conviction that, despite the horrors of Mau Mau, Kenya would soon need Kenyatta as India had needed Gandhi. After independence, he had an honoured place in East Africa.

The Booth-Clibborns returned to inner-city parishes in Lincoln. Their unusual expertise was welcomed by the British Council of Churches, Christian Aid and Lincoln Theological College. Stanley was next appointed vicar of the University Church, Great St Mary's, Cambridge. It was typical of his good humour and modesty that he would tell against himself the story of Bishop John Robinson's letter on behalf of Trinity College Patronage Committee, which pressed him to accept with the words, 'We are scraping the bottom of the barrel.'

Booth-Clibborn was 55 when appointed to the demanding diocese of Manchester. There were overwhelming problems, such as huge Victorian churches for tiny congregations, under-funded church schools and a boundary which meant that large numbers of those who drew their wealth from the city lived in and supported a neighbouring diocese. However, he was determined to 'get on with things'. He liked and admired Manchester and its civic aspects. He and Anne were endlessly kind to clergy and their families when they were in trouble, whether from vandalism, illness or a breakdown in family life.

Stanley Booth-Clibborn gave high-profile and courageous leadership wherever he was, in Kenya, Cambridge or Manchester. Speaking about the ordination of women, he said: 'Some people have interpreted episcopal leadership as meaning that the bishop should not take strong stands on controversial issues, but I think that that path simply enfeebles episcopal leadership. People respect more the kind of leadership where it is quite clear where the bishop stands.' This enabled him to agree, shortly after his appointment to Manchester, to be the first Moderator of the Movement for the Ordination of Women. His stature was recognized well beyond the diocese.

His way of working revealed his debt to his army background, both British and Salvation. He was more conservative in his faith than in his politics. Manchester felt that they had a bishop who re-sonated with much that was best in the community. A pressurized vicar put it like this: 'The bishop says his prayers and carries the burdens of his people.' In place of the old complaint, 'The Church is not for the likes of us', there came the frequent comment, 'The bishop is on our side'.

Theme 4

THE CHURCH IN ACTION

A crucial and continuing part of the Church's work is its pastoral care for its members and for the wider world. This section explores the lives of some of those who have exercised a pastoral role as church leaders, as preachers, teachers and trainers of clergy. It considers the implications of the Church's pastoral mission and the distinctive contributions made by individuals in recent years.

Cure of souls

But thou wilt sin and grief destroy;
That so the broken bones may joy
And tune together in a well-set song,
Full of his praises,
Who dead men raises.
Fractures well cured make us more strong.
George Herbert

The metaphors used in the language of Christianity include the surprising phrase 'cure of souls'. This points to a mysterious task of considering our relationships and keeping our imagination alert. If our own and each others' souls are to be cured then we need to be sensitively related to each other. Some believe that the 'soul' is an entity distinct from our bodies; others that it is the centre of our personality and of our relationships with God and each other. In the Church of Scotland the metaphors for ministry and especially for 'the charge' which is given to the newly appointed are pastoral.

Though some might not use the phrase 'cure of souls', the aim is at the heart of the modern teaching, health, social and counselling services.

The Anglican pastoral tradition was famously set out in the life, poems and essays of the seventeenth-century priest, pastor, poet and musician George Herbert. Living shortly before the Civil War disrupted the society in which he was born, he understood that suffering must be shared and mutual understanding fostered – the courage to give nothing less than life itself was needed if the deep wounds were to be healed. He saw his role as being constantly available to his parishioners, supporting them in dark days. He was a musician, never happier than when he could say to his friends, 'Let us tune our instruments'. He kept rudimentary medical supplies. The worship held in his church, in Bemerton village, always spoke of hope and resurrection.

The phrase 'cure of souls' is still used whenever a new vicar starts work. On 21 February 1953 I knelt before Michael Ramsey, then Bishop of Durham, afterwards Archbishop of Canterbury, on being appointed vicar of Barnard Castle, a North Country town of 5,000 people in Teesdale. 'Receive the cure of souls which is mine and thine' were his words. He looked searchingly into my eyes as though he was questioning as well as commissioning. R. S. Thomas, the Welsh poet-priest, in his poem 'The Empty Church', reflects on the ambiguous task of the cure of souls by those commissioned to perform it. He hoped that in some mysterious way 'someone greater than I can understand' would be revealed within the Church.

Launcelot Fleming

Launcelot Fleming's appointment by Clement Attlee in 1949 as Bishop of Portsmouth caused surprise and criticism. Fleming was 43, regarded in those days as 'young', a Trinity Hall don, an explorer and a naval chaplain in the war, but with no parochial experience, a geologist not a theologian.

The choice was inspired. Portsmouth and afterwards Norwich was given leadership intelligent, devoted and personal to the point of genius. He was not only the best of company and a cunning squash player but took unpopular stands: critical of battery farming in East Anglia, speaking in the Lords for the internationalization of the seabed when Britain depended upon North Sea oil and, long before others, firm against some of Enoch Powell's speeches. His own first speech in the Lords was to plead for the conservation of whales.

Church zealots described him as 'sexless' because he would not be pinned down in those early days of the debate against the ordination of women. He was one of the Anglican bishops in the 25 years after the war who did most to keep the Church open and tolerant, with his many friendships for men and women of different persuasions, political, scientific and religious. A small testimony of the number of his friends was the 3,000 cards he used to receive at Christmas.

At a time when the churches were in danger of retreating into themselves, Fleming stressed the need for them to listen. More perceptive than many other European bishops, Roman, Anglican or Lutheran, he realized that the number of men being ordained for full-time paid ministry was declining.

He encouraged chaplaincies of all kinds, the grouping of parishes, lay religious meetings for discussion and planning and the founding in Norwich of the ecumenical training Centre 71.

Fleming had godly Edinburgh parents and felt sufficiently at home within the Christian scheme to check it for himself. At his ordination he told his bishop that he did not accept the doctrine of the Virgin Birth. He was primarily a scientist and scientific interests grew as he got older. Struggling with the odd things worn in church he would say in the vestry of Norwich Cathedral: 'I am a liturgical rabbit.'

His unrivalled rapport with the young, including that majority who were not committed church members, led him to begin by assuring them that Christianity did not 'require them to believe ten impossible things before breakfast'. As a priest of the temple of religion with so much sympathy for those in the temple of science, he concentrated on costly simplicities – courageous offering of self for others, everyone's responsibilities for the welfare of the community, and the uniqueness and value of every single person.

Fleming's work as geologist and chaplain to the British Graham Land Expedition (1934–7) is a key to his character. His three years in the Antarctic showed him the preciousness and beauty of the planet as well as the need to respect others, especially during the harsh and dangerous journeys over the ice. Preaching to his fellow explorers in a small hut, his sermons were afterward ruthlessly pulled to pieces. 'You are a pillar of the Church and I am a buttress of hell,' said one of his listeners. In Fleming's own words, 'the fact that some cared little for the "music" of my vision makes me realize my own inadequacy . . . one drew away from the world to lonely places, there to see oneself stripped naked before the eyes of God and of one's small community of fellow men.' It was this experience which gave Fleming his unique inarticulate authority, so that school-masters and peers and parsons, those sitting on pews or in pubs, might not find a main verb to his sentences but knew they were with a person of integrity searching for truth.

His work for the Church of England was direct and practical. He advocated careful selection of ordinands, adequate payment of the clergy, and more time and energy given to lay and clerical thought and education. Especially in Norfolk he was confronted by prob-lems of isolation, loneliness, feudalism and sometimes despair. He was occasionally defeated by entrenched opposition, for instance from the members of the Chapter of St George's, Windsor, in his last post as dean. Both in Norwich and Windsor his wife Jane was his principal ally and reinforced the welcome humour and hospi-tality of their home. He believed strongly in accountability. He encouraged members of the Church to trust each other. Sport and festivities as well as conferences and seminars could exercise 'group therapy' – though he would never use those words.

He was always willing to join those outside the Church working for an open and tolerant future. One of the founders of Voluntary Service Overseas, he was an enthusiastic member of the Parliament-ary Group for World Government and a member of the Royal Commission on Environmental Pollution. As a wholly committed chaplain to the role of HMS *Queen Elizabeth* in the war he was not a pacifist, but he frequently voiced his concern over nuclear war and its unknown consequences for cancer, leukaemia and genetic muta-tion. He committed himself to the University of East Anglia as a whole, as well as to creating an ecumenical chaplaincy. He latterly gave wisdom and energy to Atlantic College, the Prince's Trust and Cathedral Camps.

Speaking to sixth formers, he insisted that it was an empirical fact that every person is unique. Religion should begin here and go further. Our faith impels us, whatever the disadvantage to ourselves, to be committed to each other's welfare, to relationships where humour and warmth, as well as wisdom and courage, can knit us together. Scientists and believers must combine empirical concern for the facts with the religious concern for committed relationships.

Fleming was to the end concerned to align his beliefs to ultimate truth. He felt in the years of his retirement that his final message was 'Be natural – don't pose – be yourself and look this way . . . For me, that means looking to Jesus Christ, though not to Him alone, so as to try to understand and respond better to the wonder and mystery of God's creation and purpose.'

Fleming's vision and practice made him unique among bishops in the post-war Church.

Kenneth Riches

The close encounters at Lincoln Cathedral, which were dramatized by the media in the 1990s, have obscured the achievements of the long episcopate of Kenneth Riches (1956–74).

His colleagues included some of the ablest Anglican priests of the time: Dick Milford, the theologian who founded Oxfam; Colin Dunlop, the dean who invited Duncan Grant to create his unusual chapel; and Oliver Tomkins, the leading ecumenist, to mention but three.

Lay people trusted Riches and found that they could be much more outspoken to him than to many bishops. When he consulted a Lincolnshire farmer about the appointment of a priest and family from Zimbabwe, he was rewarded with honesty – ''e couldn't be wuss than some of the white 'uns we've 'ad.' He had time to laugh and to believe the best of people. Riches was an East Anglian, educated at Colchester Royal Grammar School and Corpus Christi College, Cambridge, where he took a First in Theology. Perhaps he might have become a rather black-suited priest, but from his days as a curate at Portsea, as a Cambridge chaplain, and as a Suffolk country clergyman, he continued to grow in tolerance, sympathy and wit. His marriage to Katharine Dixon was a total success. Her common sense, helpfulness and hard work never let the episcopal side of his life go to his head. After a time as Principal of Cuddesdon (1945–52), where the regime was relaxed and the students, many of them straight from war service, could be themselves, Riches was briefly a suffragan bishop before he was appointed to Lincoln.

Like most post-war Lincolnshire people, whether farmers, industrialists, teachers or local government leaders, Riches worked for moderate change. He was a friend of other churches, and a strong supporter of Archbishop Ramsey's efforts to bring Anglicans and Methodists together again. He did not hesitate to speak in the Church Assembly in favour of removing the bar to women's ordination. He empathized with the problems of tiny parishes who felt their individuality as strongly as if their Danish founders had only left yesterday, and created the famous South Ormsby Group – linking 14 small parishes – which was copied in other dioceses. He did not neglect the considerable problems of Scunthorpe, and welcomed clergy from the diocese of Sheffield, then suffering from reactionary leadership, and began industrial mission in the steel works. He was diligent in supporting more traditional parishes in Lincoln, Grimsby, Sleaford and Grantham and was prepared to bring in pioneering priests, such as Stanley Booth-Clibborn, to create a city centre parish. His cathedral, college and diocese became happy and confident.

Working at Lincoln Theological College from 1959 to 1970, I found him a supportive and imaginative chairman. Together with the lay leaders on the college's council, he approved a series of staff appointments unusual in Anglican theological colleges: Methodist and Roman Catholic scholars and Peggy Hartley, a lecturer in social work. He supported the policy of buying houses for married students so that their families could be integrated into the life of the college and the city. My successor in 1970 was able to admit women for training into the college itself. In the new atmosphere of the

1960s, after *Honest to God* (that radical explanation of faith by Bishop John Robinson) and the departure of so many priests and religious from the Roman Catholic Church, it was refreshing to work with a bishop who did not wring his hands and murmur 'Better not'. He was unfussy, prepared to think and then say what he thought. Even if his overcrowded diary led to some double bookings, people smiled rather than swore and said, 'the unsearchable riches'.

It is fair to ask whether the later turmoil at Lincoln Cathedral, and the closure of the college, could have been avoided. Certainly Riches would have prevented patronage secretaries in London making foolish appointments. But he allowed the antiquated Cathedral Statutes to remain unreformed. Perhaps the glamour of antiquity was too influential. It would be fairer to say that the pastoral care of his enormous diocese, as well as his duties in London, which included the chairmanship of the ministry committee of the church, and his tasks as visitor of colleges and schools outside his diocese, were too overwhelming to enable him to devote energy to reforms – reforms which might have prevented the crises which arose ten years after his time.

In retirement at Dunwich he and Katharine, who had given so much service to so many good causes, were happy and hospitable. Their house and garden, hidden in woods but within sound of the sea, welcomed old friends and old students from many eras of his ministry. His knowledge of furniture, his faithfully undertaken retreats and his mature, smiling, spiritual life led many to visit him in eastern England, where he was at home.

Edward Patey

Edward Patey, who died aged 90, was Dean of Liverpool from 1964 until 1982. 'Ed Patey' or 'Matey Patey', as Scouse humorists nicknamed him, was once introduced by the late Brian Redhead, on BBC radio, as the man 'who looks after the only unfinished ancient monument in the country'.

The wealthy merchants with so much civic pride in their booming city, who had created the Anglican diocese in 1880 and laid the foundation stone of Giles Gilbert Scott's cathedral on St James' Mount in 1904, would have been startled that 60 years later the vast Gothic building, one of the world's largest, would not only be unfinished but the object of public debate: could a shrinking church in a disturbed city find any use for such a building?

Patey arrived from the South but came to be forgiven for not being a Liverpudlian, thanks to his humanity and hard work. They welcomed his decision to spend half his working time on public non-church bodies, race relations, unemployment projects and the troubles of Toxteth. Old-fashioned clerics were taken aback by the ordinariness of the Pateys' deanery; his wife Margaret was later awarded an OBE for social work. Visiting preachers from more orderly cities expressed surprise when their vehicles, secure in the cathedral car park, were rifled. Patey, whose tall, dishevelled figure was often seen on a battered bike, would twit them for their ignorance of Britain as it had become, and laughingly help them replace what was lost.

Patey was the son of a Bristol doctor and educated at Marlborough School, Hertford College, Oxford, and Westcott House, Cambridge, where he prepared for holy orders. He was ordained in 1939.

He was influenced by the Student Christian Movement, the British and World Councils of Churches and by inner-city parish experience in Colchester from 1939 to 1942, Sunderland from 1942 to 1950, and Bristol from 1950 until 1952. Having been an outstanding youth chaplain to the Bishop of Durham from 1946, he was Secretary to the Youth Department of the British Council of Churches (BCC) from 1952 to 1955. He was then Assistant General Secretary of the BCC until 1958, when he was appointed Canon Residentiary at Coventry Cathedral.

At Coventry he had first-hand experience of finishing a cathedral, working with a highly motivated and forward-looking team and cooperating with a left-wing local authority. The sheer heaviness of the Anglican establishment was held in check as Coventry was rebuilt. Cooperation with Europe, the English Free Churches, and with the largely unchurched teenagers in the schools and colleges of the Midlands, hardened Patey's convictions that the ecclesiastical topics of how to stop reunion or silence women offering for ordination or whether worship should be high or low were unimportant compared with, to use the title of his last book, *Faith in a Risk-Taking God* (1991). Patey always refrained from pietistic polemics and preached for radical reform, especially on Vatican II lines.

As a fluent, frequent speaker and writer – he published 20 books, many designed to assist study groups – he was ahead of other church leaders in detecting the changes of the 1960s. While Anglican official teaching still spoke of 'living in sin' when discussing pre-marital sex, Patey's *Young People Now* (1964) documented convictions about morality and relationships among the 1960s generation. He foreshadowed the Synod report *Something to Celebrate* (1995) by 30 years. He also foresaw the near-universal plea for intercommunion between the denominations.

Some of his friends tried to dissuade him from leaving Coventry for what the radical church journal *New Christian* described as the 'Liverpool folly' and the *Guardian* as the 'Gothic obsolescent Cathedral Church of Christ'. Even more daunting were the vastly rising costs in days of runaway inflation, strikes, vandalism and theft on the site and a breakdown at the Cumbria quarry. But Patey became a powerful leader, support was rallied among rich and poor and, though there was still scaffolding and no great west door, the Queen opened the nearly complete cathedral in October 1978. She was the fourth member and fourth generation of the royal family to visit the cathedral at a crucial moment.

Patey's imaginative faith and his popularity frequently filled the 4,000 places with children and young people. In 1981, the John Lennon memorial service and in 1982, the visits of Archbishop Robert Runcie and, later that year, John Paul II, all caused controversy, but it was miraculous that it was in Liverpool of all places that these tolerant and ecumenical foundations were laid. In 1974 a full-time ecumenical officer was appointed for Merseyside on the grounds that in Patey's words, 'A divided church can win no credibility in preaching reconciliation to a divided community . . . This is not window dressing. It is basic Christianity.' With the enthusiastic support of Bishop David Sheppard and his colleagues, especially the gifted canon Basil Naylor, Patey left Liverpool Cathedral as one of the warmest and most open-hearted of the cathedrals of any church today.

Preaching in retirement in 1993 at the Winchester Cathedral 900th anniversary celebrations, Patey continued to look to the future:

> Cathedrals must be seen and used by all sorts of people, not as a closed shop but as an open house. The staff should include women, non-Anglicans and lay people, all not by 'kind permission of the Dean and Chapter' but by right as fellow workers in the Cause.

He saw cathedrals with their standards in music, art and erudition as rescuing us from Mickey Mouse religion, not playing safe but prepared to take risks in prophecy and preaching. Patey had always been a pioneer and he remained one to the end.

Francis House

The Venerable Francis House, who has died aged 96, was one of the unsung heroes of the Church of England's work in rescuing persecuted Christians and Jews from Hitler's Europe. His courage, linguistic abilities and sense of justice made him a trusted agent for numerous dangerous journeys, both as a student and a priest, throughout the 1930s. Ordained in 1937, he worked for the BBC during the war, later becoming Head of Religious Broadcasting.

Born in Almondbury, near Huddersfield, House was brought up in Essex, where his father was a vicar. He was educated at St George's School, Harpenden, and Wadham College, Oxford, where he read Modern Greats from 1927 to 1930. After university, he became secretary of the Student Christian Movement (SCM) and began to visit Central Europe, on one occasion infiltrating a Nazi youth training camp in East Prussia. This was a time when there was virulent anti-semitism in some Central European universities, and still some sympathy in England for Hitler.

After training at Cuddesdon Theological College, Oxford, House joined the Pembroke College Mission at Walworth, south London, in 1935. He continued, however, to visit Germany, making contact with opposition friends, sometimes at a secret forest rendezvous, an art gallery in Munich or at the Berlin zoo. Back in England, he reported the dangers facing liberal Germans to the Archbishop of Canterbury, William Temple, and the Bishop of Chichester, George Bell.

In 1938, House was appointed as Travelling Secretary of the World Student Christian Federation, in Geneva. Newly married, he and his wife, Margaret Neave, also an able linguist, set off to contact student movements in the Balkans, threatened as war preparations began. He also visited Berlin to meet leaders of the Young Church movement, soon to be imprisoned for supporting the Jews. He was in Germany in 1938, at the time of Kristallnacht, and in Vienna when the German army arrived in 1938.

House did his best to persuade the church authorities that Hitler was a menace. In spite of Vatican opposition, he was able to meet the secretary of Pax Romana, the Roman Catholic student organization, to coordinate plans to rescue students opposed to the Nazis, whether Catholic, Orthodox or Protestant.

In 1940, House returned to England, where he served on the staff of Leeds parish church. With Russian now among his languages, he was chosen to organize the wartime journey of Archbishop Cyril Garbett of York to Moscow – the first official visit by a non-Orthodox churchman to Russia since the 1917 revolution.

In 1942, the BBC recognized House's unusual qualities and appointed him as producer of religious broadcasts to Germany. He insisted that the broadcasts, from Bush House, should be religion and not propaganda. Once, he recreated a padre's sermon from Bethlehem, where the quality was so terrible that, in House's words, 'a camel must have been trampling on the landline'. Governments-in-exile in London welcomed him at their chaplains' group, which planned for post-war cooperation.

After post-war relief work in Greece with the United Nations Relief and Rehabilitation Administration (UNRRA) and further service in Geneva, House returned to London to become the BBC's Head of Religious Broadcasting (1947–55). His administrative efficiency and strict impartiality between denominations were valued, and when television came on stream, the religious department was expanded. The televising of Elizabeth II's coronation was a triumph, and persuaded many clergy hostile to television that this was something with which the churches could live.

House also prepared the way for religion on commercial television, arguing strongly that the churches should not 'buy time', and that the central religious advisory committee should be consulted by both the BBC and commercial television.

House did a further spell at Geneva, with the newly created World Council of Churches, and returned home to become vicar of Pontefract, West Yorkshire, and later of Gawsworth, Cheshire. To many, this was curious, but Archbishop Michael Ramsey was slow to recognize the abilities of those who had worked outside England. Eventually, Gerald Ellison, Bishop of Chester, appointed him Archdeacon of Macclesfield (1967–78), and he became Vice-Chairman of the Board of Mission and Unity. He made valuable visits to Burundi and Madagascar, and assisted Archbishop Ramsey in the ecumenical approaches to the Methodist Church.

When, however, a new Bishop of Chester, who hated ecumenism, was appointed, House resigned. He enjoyed a long and creative retirement in Leeds. He continued to work for ecumenism, published an illustrated account of Christianity in Russia and was a strong supporter of the ordination of women.

Frank Wright

Frank Wright devoted his ministry to rethinking Christian teaching and reanimating the lifestyle of Christian communities, especially in the north of England. As Sub-Dean of Manchester Cathedral, adviser to Granada Television and an extra-mural lecturer at Manchester University, he was influential with the leaders of the churches in Lancashire and had a bold vision of what the Church might be in British society.

As a keynote speaker at conferences and producer of ITV religious programmes he insisted, despite protests from those who wanted to press the traditional religion of standards and law, that the love of God was unconditional. He urged a fresh philosophy for Christian communication.

Frank Wright was born at Orrell, near Wigan, in 1922 and educated at Upholland Grammar School. He remained loyal to Lancashire, including Lancashire cricket at Old Trafford. From Upholland he went to St Peter's Hall, Oxford, to study Modern History, and on to Second World War service in the RAF. As a Beaufighter navigator, sent to attack a ship in Preveza harbour in Greece, his mission ended with two years as a POW at Muhlberg.

He discovered his inner resources, which enabled survival at the heights and depths of cut-throat selfishness (well described in his *Invisible Network: The Story of Air Care*, 1989). From his prison he could see the contrast between his camp and a chaotic prison 30 yards away for Russians and Poles and the nearby German town, whose citizens seemed wholly indifferent. His powers of attention as friend or pastor, lecturer or television producer were learnt in this tough school. He always gave you the whole of his attention.

After training at Westcott House, Cambridge, with other ex-service students, he was ordained at Durham. Curacies at Sunderland and Barnard Castle showed he was determined to change the old order so that parish churches might be agents of 'unconditional caring in the community', to quote a favourite phrase. He was highly original as Rector of Stretford, Manchester (1955–66), forming a 24-strong group of lay carers concerned for people whether churchgoers or not; he was critical of many stewardship campaigns which suggested to outsiders that the Church's motives were financial and statistical. He opposed (obstinately, some of his fellow clergy thought) all forms of institutional publicity and self-concern. In his sermons and later broadcasts he liked to remind people of the early church, which turned the world upside down, when its possessions and buildings were almost nil and all its members were highly vulnerable.

From 1966 he worked from Manchester Cathedral, but was also Honorary Lecturer in Pastoral Theology at Manchester University, and religious adviser to Granada Television in Lancashire. Wright published six books on pastoral care much valued by clergy of different denominations. Of these *The Pastoral Nature of Ministry* (1980) and *The Pastoral Nature of Healing* (1985) were particularly appreciated. He visited Toulouse (twinned with Manchester), as well as New York and Canada, in search of good practice in pastoral care. His *Exploration into Goodness* (1988) revealed the breadth of his reading and his admiration for those who searched for truth without being members of the Church, particularly Iris Murdoch, Simone Weil and Albert Camus. Despite his many commitments Wright had the gift of staying in touch with those he taught. I discovered members of St Paul's Cathedral congregation who were still in correspondence with him years after the retreat when they first met.

Granada Television, encouraged by their chairman Sir Denis Forman, gave Wright exceptional opportunities by asking him to produce hour-long meditations, which were networked. His programmes drew on the experience of joy and hope, failure and guilt, the approach of death, the diminishment of poverty and unemployment. Wright insisted that there was no short cut to goodness. He introduced some of the most challenging contemporary theologians and writers – David Jenkins, Monica Furlong, Don Cupitt – as well as poets and novelists. Moments of silence, visits to beautiful places of prayer such as Taizé and a Roman Catholic retreat centre, with meticulously chosen music, created compelling meditations. Counsellors were available on the telephone and to reply to letters.

Wright's individualistic grittiness, and the ill-health he suffered following his POW days, led him to say no to efforts to appoint him Bishop of Manchester. His constantly supportive wife, Peggy, made their home, latterly at Brampton, near Carlisle, a honeypot for visitors and enquirers. He was able to share with so many his humour, love of music and literature, and his pride in his three children and their achievements, but he never lost the private and reserved elements in his character.

Even when seriously lame and unable to drive he would find his way to celebrate Holy Communion in a parish church. He remained a pattern pastor, empathetic to what was vulnerable in the faith lives of others, much respected for his independence of mind and integrity.

John Tinsley

John Tinsley was a scholar-bishop of unusual acumen and sensitivity. For him the bishop's *cathedra* was always the chair of a teacher available and encouraging to those who listened. While Bishop of Bristol, from 1976 to 1985, he was happier sitting on the edge of a table rather than robed in the pulpit six feet above query or contradiction. He stretched his hearers, gave them the licence to think for themselves, to question and to doubt.

Obviously hesitant, he won the respect of many outsiders, including those producing television programmes and the Home Office committee on obscenity and film censorship on which he served (1977–9). His academic work on the complex story of Christian attempts at 'the imitation of Christ' and his freedom from any form of ecclesiastical double-speak gave a mature stature to his nine years on the bishops' bench. He remained available to enquirers and friends until his final illness.

Tinsley, the son of a Lancashire farmer, was born in 1919 and educated and ordained at Durham. He and his wife Marjorie were at home in the north of England. As a lecturer at Hull University he worked to build up an autonomous theological department between 1946 and 1961. He was Professor of Theology at Leeds University from 1961 to 1975. His students caught his delight in the visual and his sense of God as artist, even if this occasionally meant just too many slides to illustrate Byzantine iconography and Romanesque architecture.

All his days he retained the good don's ability to see those who wanted to talk far into the night, even if the subject was their own follies. His belief in the divine gift of freedom increased the sense of trust so many experienced when he was their professor, examiner or bishop.

Emily Dickinson's injunction 'Tell it slant' early caught his attention. His northern common sense, fortified by his deep knowledge of Continental theology, rejected the notion that the imitation of Christ is an endeavour to mimic the historical Jesus. Instead, he drew attention to Søren Kierkegaard's distinction between 'admiration' and 'imitation'. He urged the Church to find a contemporary 'yes' to God in faith and total commitment.

In his thinking as an educationalist and an evangelist, Tinsley opposed all forms of manipulation. For him, divine revelation itself, as in the incarnation of Christ, was not direct but allusive, parabolic and persuasive. Archdeacons and other close friends would pass on to him that people found him hard to follow. His diffident but firm teaching ministry only gradually persuaded those who had relied on the fundamentalism of creed or the scriptural text. He pointed to something more profound than they had yet grasped. Bristol heads, originally nodding out of courtesy or slumber, began to experience their faith as a reality beyond words.

Both the city and the Church in Bristol could be against change. Tinsley believed that 'A bishop is charged to experiment and take risks.' He faced opposition over the reorganization of the historic city-centre churches. He also had plans for the needs, especially educational, of the housing estates and inner-city areas such as St Paul's. He faced a flood of protests. He did not retreat but remarked with a determined twinkle, 'The idea that religion does not mix with politics is a very English way of sitting on the fence.' He carried the reorganization of the city churches to the Privy Council and won.

His concern for more resources for education, both for the young and for adults, was central to his ministry. He served at Church House as Chairman of the Synodical Board of Education. In addition he argued strongly that the bars to women in the Church should be removed. All this was costly to someone who read and considered all the letters he received. He was a reforming bishop, resisting the temptation to appease and soothe.

The Church also gave him the ecumenical task of negotiation with German Lutherans, to whom he was drawn through his knowledge of Luther and Bonhoeffer. These negotiations have now resulted in the Meissen Agreement between Anglicans and Lutherans. The loneliness and sorrow he experienced over the death of his beloved wife Marjorie, and his long widowerhood, may well have deepened the quality of his pastoral care.

He enjoyed his family and friends and, being a Francophile, extracted enormous pleasure from holidays in the Auvergne, Alsace, Paris and especially Bordeaux, with which Bristol is linked. Wearing a black beret with a tassel, he slipped light-heartedly into France.

John Tinsley, his writings and teaching, influenced many more people than he ever realized. Alert, shy, orthodox-minded yet liberal, he once expressed his faith in these measured words: 'God is not at the disposal of our reason, our imagination or our emotion; we are at His.'

Joan Ramsey

All those who care for strong leadership in Christianity, both in England and in the Anglican Communion, are in debt to Joan Ramsey. Without her it would have been impossible for anyone so shy, donnish and profound as Michael Ramsey to have become one of the most travelled and wisest Archbishops of Canterbury. It was a triumph of two diffident people; friends had expected neither of them to marry. Yet they were so in love and so in tune with each other that their service to their country and their Church was outstanding.

Joan Ramsey became an intelligent and welcoming hostess in the succession of those who have set out to humanize and warm those formidable episcopal houses of Auckland Castle, Bishopthorpe and Lambeth Palace. She had a genius for putting people at ease, much needed when the archbishop had lapsed into one of his silent reveries. With her startling memory, piquant humour and smiling, enquiring face she gave a special attraction to the archbishop's many receptions and journeys.

Born Joan Hamilton, she had a clerical grandfather and uncle and knew the Church well enough to be able to laugh at it and yet share its inner face with confidence. She met Michael Ramsey in 1940 when he came from posts at Lincoln Theological College and Cambridge to be Canon and Professor of Divinity at Durham University. He did not drive a car; she did. Joan knew County Durham well and they were married in the cathedral in 1942.

In 1950 she made the first of their many moves and house renovations, going to Cambridge when he was appointed Regius Professor of Divinity. They returned after only two years to Durham, but this time to Auckland Castle, when Michael was appointed bishop. While Michael rejoiced in the history and spirituality of the castle and its chapels, Joan had to cope with the unique non-system of passages, staircases, cooking arrangements and the famous butler of that complex and exceedingly expensive pile.

Especially at Durham, but also at York and Lambeth and Canterbury, she devoted her life to making Michael and those who worked with him happy. If she called on a vicarage in Teesdale it seemed natural to take her to the kitchen and not hurry to light a fire in the drawing-room. She enjoyed political gossip and jokes and her own conversation could be acerbic, puncturing pomposity. Once at Lambeth Palace, grabbing a friend to move a wedged dining-room table, she remarked: 'Lambeth is the smallest house we have lived in.'

Both were old-fashioned; she admired but laughed at the Cambridge side of the archbishop. She never gave an interview herself. She encouraged Michael to speak out, remembering he had been president of the Union. She shared his anger over South African apartheid. She encouraged him to face the authorities there and the frequent indifference of parts of the London establishment. She was beside him in every sense during his deep depression over the clerical intolerance which defeated his hopes of reunion with the Methodist Church.

Joan Ramsey endured much ill-health and they both grieved that they had no children. She enjoyed simply being beside him and he died in her arms. Her faith was rooted in the sacraments. She will enjoy the good company of heaven.

Village churches

Village churches with tiny congregations do not make much of a showing in the sociology and statistics of religion, but they witness uniquely to concern for the Spirit in the countryside. Among the tiny shrines of the north none is more memorable than the chapel at Cartmell Fell, built about 1500 and rare among ancient churches in the north-west in being dedicated to St Anthony, the saint of the monks of the desert in Egypt; the hermit who died in 356 and led the campaign against superficial living in the cities. This tiny chapel is off the beaten track, surrounded by trees and in spring by myriads of dwarf daffodils, the Lent lilies immortalized by the Lake poets.

Cartmell Fell has a host of unorganized pilgrims who make their way from the cities to this fresh spring of spirituality and prayer.

Typical were Alan and Delia Ecclestone, who worked for decades in the east end of Sheffield. Alan was in many ways prophetic, if not revolutionary. But it was to this tiny, quiet holy place that he returned. These shrines are places for reflection, prayer and recovery of vision. As the psalmist puts it: 'All my fresh springs shall be in Thee' (Ps. 87.7).

Another out-of-the-way shrine is at Ormside. Orm was a Viking who probably arrived around 915, the year the Danes pillaged York. So this church began as a pagan burial ground on its impressive hill, where excavations have unearthed the great treasure of the Ormside Bowl and a Viking sword. The people used their revered burial ground to erect their church and also used it as a school. The sense of struggle down the centuries in remote dales is reinforced by the display in the church of the Will of the Black Prince, which was written by the priest of Ormside in 1376, possibly when the prince was on his way to Scotland. A later priest of Ormside, Joseph Brunskill, who died there in 1903, tried to persuade Cumberland farmers to let the children of the poor have some of their milk and caused no little ill will by riding to farms to argue the point. When the tilting express train crashed in the night at the Westmorland village of Grayrigg in 2007, it was the village community which opened its doors to the shattered and wounded travellers.

The Scottish and French countryside also has many of these tiny churches. No village church is more beautifully sited than Kincraig on its tree-guarded hill by the loch. Though Presbyterian, its pulpit has a Bible which records its gratitude to K. M. Carey, a bishop in another church who occasionally prayed and preached there and was a friend of many in Kincraig. Near Cahors in southern France is the small medieval church of Maxou, recently expertly restored by the French government. So few priests are now available for rural France that it must share very occasional services with more than twenty other villages, but an English couple have been given the keys to open and close it and, though Protestant, they are invited to receive Communion at Maxou. Village churches with a strong sense of community can overcome the divisions caused by ecclesiastical triumphalism and disputes down the centuries.

Mallerstang, hidden in its valley near Kirkby Stephen, like so many of these small shrines, owes much to the faith of women. Lady Anne Clifford (1590–1676), as an inscription over the porch records, was a principal benefactor and builder. Her chapel was used as a school in the nineteenth century as well as a centre for worship and the community gathered round it cared as much as it could for the harshly treated railway workers building the Midland line to the north. The burial registers show how many left their bones in the valley.

In the 1920s after the First World War, the working days at the Cheshire village of Wrenbury included the church bell ringing at 9 a.m. One morning I decided to find out what my father, the vicar, did after he had rung the bell. Crawling through the gaps under the pews I wriggled unseen to the front and heard extraordinary language. He was saying the psalms in Hebrew aloud, and defended this odd practice, as I saw it, by saying, 'After all, they were written in Hebrew.' He also read them in Hebrew when visiting Jewish patients in the local TB sanatorium. When a young man in the village lost his sight because the lime he was slaking in a milk churn flew up in his face, my father and the leading Methodist went round in those pre-welfare state days to collect enough to have him retrained, given a weekly allowance and a shoe repair shop in which to work. 'Thou shalt love thy neighbour as thyself.'

Theme 5

ENRICHING HUMAN LIFE

This group of articles brings together two other means of enhancing human life: the provision of health care and the work of creative artists and performers. They can be perceived as working in complementary ways. Both can lead to reflection on the human condition. Medicine has its creative aspect and the arts have a therapeutic and uplifting effect. Both have their impact in improving the quality of our lives.

All shall be well

Every year 40,000 people undergo total hip replacement, one of the most successful items in the modern medical repertoire. Naturally, when you are to receive one yourself, you ask questions about dates. Last year I received the reply 'April 2003'. I was delighted that it was not further away and that I would have the summer months to regain mobility, but I realized I would be in London in hospital for Easter. What would it feel like to be deprived of all the usual services of Holy Week and Easter, not to join the crowds who throng the churches and cathedrals?

My fears of loneliness were banished by nearest and dearest, family and friends and members of the congregations where I had worshipped. The cost to them in effort, time and practical imagination were all testimonies to that New Testament insistence that we visit the sick, and be as alert as Christ to their needs. A lay friend bent his journey from Westminster to Fleet Street to bring a bottle of champagne on the day of my operation. The family put it in a fridge and brought it back to celebrate Easter Day at a tiny party with a fellow patient and two grandchildren.

One of the hospital's stated aims was to establish a personal relationship between staff and patients. What did I want to be called? They seemed to expect a job description and a first name so we settled on 'Dean Alan'. As the mists of anaesthetic faded I tried to remember their names, amazingly various from all the world's continents, thanks to the globalization of modern nursing.

A nurse from the Caribbean told me of the two children she is bringing up in the East End while her doctor husband is working in the States. Nurses from Namibia, India, South Africa, Brazil, New Zealand, all came to care. It felt as if our Western internationalized medical service was fulfilling Christ's dream of universal caring love. But undeveloped countries are still desperately short. The events of Good Friday and Easter were believed by the Church to have cosmic significance and Christ himself came to be called *Salvator mundi*.

Post-operation euphoria wears off and sleep can be elusive. Visits from surgeon and anaesthetist, two blood transfusions and the hydro pool were restorative, but the 'black dog' of depression was also an occasional visitor. Would I ever enjoy walking or swimming again? My leg seemed not to belong to me and I resented its ineffectiveness. Oddly, I felt strengthened by remembering how much religious teaching is negative. I remembered those disciples left in total despair and profound hopelessness on the road to Emmaus. Reading and, even more, writing failed me. The radio, especially Mark Tully's *Something Understood* from New Delhi, helped, with its poetry and music and the sense of a subconscious spirituality from the Psalms and the Prayer Book.

Later, I found Dr Oliver Sacks' *A Leg to Stand On* a rich resource. He quotes John Donne – 'I am re-begot by Absence, Darkness, Death; things which are not' – as well as the philosopher David Hume's conviction about our perceptions being in 'a perpetual flux and movement'. I found myself, like Dr Sacks, addressing an 'unimaginable Thou', comforted by a mysterious presence.

Both hospitals had chaplains; gentle, sensitive men closely linked to the healing and counselling professions in their London areas, and they seemed to have time. They brought the Sacrament on four or five occasions in that fortnight, and the Holy Week and Easter readings added an intensity of concern with life and death. We remembered a fellow patient who had had a hysterectomy and was returning home to care for a husband suffering from Alzheimer's. The crisis in Iraq was developing and many health workers were Muslim. I felt the ancient words 'Lift up your hearts' with a new sense of appreciation for the healing services and the miraculous caring of loved ones, family and friends.

When I returned home, thanks to the benign road transport of a volunteer from the Red Cross, it was some time before I could rejoin the churchgoers. Then it was with eight others at a weekday communion in a country church. The celebrant asked me to give the New Testament reading. Two sticks and a fifteenth-century pillar got me to and kept me on my feet, as well as the faith and friendship of the congregation. Since it was May – the month of Julian of Norwich – I recalled her words that 'All shall be well and all shall be well and all manner of thing shall be well.'

When Holy Week and Easter come in 2004 I'm sure I'll have religious as well as medical reasons for my gratitude for those weeks barred from church attendance by a stay in hospital. My hospital intuitions will fuse with the worship of the Church and enrich my perceptions. Perhaps we need times of abstinence from the over-familiar religious words to grasp the realities to which they point.

A stay in hospital is a lesson in the meaning and value of trust

When leaving hospital recently I was struck by the notice on the fresh brickwork: 'The Norfolk and Norwich University Hospital NHS Trust'.

In the creation of this complex new institution, a great variety of bodies and groups had to trust each other. It was not merely the city – a city with a history of producing radicals and pioneers – and the young university, whose medical faculty is still being created.

The hospital's success depends on many institutions, including the state itself, being able to rely on each other's intelligent faith in humanity's duty to cure and to heal. It depends on the trust of the whole community.

Trust can be difficult. We cannot always even hear, as the north-country actress Thora Hird once observed. She thought she was asking an elderly patient her name, but the patient thought Hird was asking what her illness was.

'Renal colic,' she said.

'That's an odd name,' said Hird. 'Renal colic, you must be French!'

They were all at sixes and sevens but both roared with laughter. To trust each other requires all the sensitive humanity we possess. Often the technical medical language is obscure, and those who study communication in hospitals deserve our gratitude. Conversation in a globalized health service can be complicated – hence, among other things, the popularity of Joy Parkinson's manual for overseas staff in our contemporary NHS. Trust in the reliability of hospitals takes time to grow but is needed urgently in the new generation of hospitals.

One Sunday I was wheeled down the long corridors and through the lifts to join a score of others in the chapel.

I was handed a small, chunky, wooden cross from Africa. The celebrant was a priest who was also a nurse. Her address at the eucharist revealed that she had recently returned from working with tsunami victims of different nationalities and faiths. She reminded us that we live in a suffering world and share the experience of underdeveloped nations unable to provide Western facilities.

On one of my corridor journeys I was pushed by my 12-year-old grandson, under the eye of the staff; you can't start too young when learning about trust, and hospitals can be laboratories of trust.

Ancient hospitals have known generations of trust. The Great Hospital at Norwich, founded in 1249, had an unbroken record of trust between different professions. Down the centuries people doctored and nursed, cooked, cleaned, paid the wages, endowed funds for enlargement and rebuilding and heard those words, 'I was sick and you visited me'.

Founded by a bishop at home in London, Oxford, Rome and Paris, its post-Reformation friends included a leader of the Congregational Church, imprisoned for his views. Fortunately, he was released by Robert Cecil, Queen Elizabeth's chief minister, who wanted tolerance.

Two centuries later enlightened philanthropists were inspired to buy some of its land to found the first Norfolk and Norwich Hospital.

The NHS is trust on a grand scale. It now has around a million staff – it is the country's largest employer. Taxation and contributions through national insurance payments ensure that we all pay for each other – on the principle of the Good Samaritan.

But for all the legislative requirements of what Archbishop William Temple called 'the welfare state', and for all the amazing technology and skills of contemporary hospitals, we still need the upholding presence of personal care. The long nights when illness feels hideous, and isolation and depression cloud the mind, make us all the more alert to those who bring that sense of wholeness which is medicine for the soul.

Rogues of profit still haunt the celestial road

Mr Valiant-for-Truth is such an old-fashioned name that we do not expect it in a science laboratory, on a twenty-first-century website or in a modern office. Perhaps we should look harder.

William Anderson, newly employed in 1987 at the London offices of the Wellcome Trust, noticed an urn high up on a top shelf. Anderson, an inquisitive scholar who had written on Dante, Gothic architecture and the Green Man, discovered that the urn contained the ashes of the founder, Sir Henry Wellcome (1853–1936). His body had been cremated 50 years earlier but there had been no agreement on the disposal of his ashes. Anderson organized their burial in the churchyard of St Paul's Cathedral, where a memorial was later erected, with recognition of a man who is now remembered in the crypt of St Paul's alongside Florence Nightingale and Sir Alexander Fleming. He is described as 'Pharmacist and

Philanthropist, Patron of medical research and history and Founder of the Wellcome Trust'.

The trust is now the world's largest charity for medical research. Born in his grandfather's log cabin in Wisconsin, Wellcome escaped poverty through his skill as a pharmacist and in 1889 moved to London with his colleague Silas Burroughs. He became interested in pure research and in the mass production of many major drugs, including anti-diphtheria, insulin and what later became anti-Aids medicines. He supported the Gordon Memorial College at Khartoum and other medical missionary responses to diseases, and was active in fighting the malaria crisis when the Panama Canal was constructed. His involvement when he was nine in the bloody Sioux rising gave him deep sympathy for Native Americans, for whom he was a persistent advocate. Though he died enormously rich, with collections larger than those in the Louvre and the British Museum, his latest biographer believes 'he was genuinely more interested in pure research than in the commercial benefits that might accrue'.

The Watson and Crick discoveries in molecular biology, with DNA as a basic substance influencing heredity, and the subsequent human genome project at 20 worldwide laboratories (in England at the Sanger Centre near Cambridge), have been among the crucial scientific quests of the present day. Craig Venter in the US wished to work through company activity, but John Sulston and the British team preferred to remain in the public sphere, open to the world's scholars. In 1995 the Wellcome Trust committed itself to such generous support of the Sanger Centre that this public project was preserved from private commercialization. Some see this as a crucial decision made by British scientists for the world's freedom of knowledge; others argue that only the market can pay for the necessary experimental work.

Perhaps Mr Valiant-for-Truth matters as much in the laboratory, on the Internet and in the market as he did in *The Pilgrim's Progress*. Difficult judgements on issues of great complexity about patenting, publication and access face those concerned with research. The magazine *Nature* has argued that it is unfair to see scientists as motivated by short-term financial gain. They face dilemmas.

In the past 50 years Nelson Mandela has become the world's Mr Valiant-for-Truth, saying that free drugs and vaccinations are needed by millions of the world's children. Botched research when the needs are so great is like an encyclopaedia ripped to shreds and scattered on the floor. To see fresh discoveries as gifts to all humanity and as sources of respect rather than financial profit should be the aim of the world's governments and trusts.

Among scientific giants such as America, India and China, our small island can be led by scientists who are Valiant-for-Truth; then the trumpets will sound 'on the farther side'. We need our leaders – political, religious and academic – to trumpet the necessity for the world's scientists to unite to fight malaria, Aids and children's diseases. Can our leaders declare a moratorium on political, credal and racial disputes and turn simply to human need?

Much must still be discovered. The time has come, especially for religious leaders, to concentrate the minds of humanity on ordinary worldwide suffering, the need for tolerance of different cultures, and to share the deep ills of creation.

Threefold cord of religion, science and literature in the character of Sir Thomas Browne

The tercentenary, Browne 300, inspired from the Norfolk and Norwich Hospital, provides an incentive in an age of intense specialization to review the achievement of a great doctor who pursued a different course and fused in himself three major disciplines. In his commonplace book he describes how the bones from the charnel house of St Paul's, more than a thousand cartloads, were transported to Finsbury Fields when the ground was being prepared to build the new St Paul's by Christopher Wren, another comprehensive genius, whose birth 350 years ago we are also commemorating this year. The whole of old St Paul's was cleared, partly by gunpowder, and the bones from the charnel house, the site of the present crypt, were transported to Finsbury Fields, 'and there laid in a moorish place with so much soil to cover them as raised the ground for three windmills which have since been built there, grinding food for the living on the bones of the dead'.[1] Our prayer today is that the dry bones of Sir Thomas Browne may receive the breath of the spirit so that we share his zest for life, his special sense of humour and happiness – in other words, bread for our living in the twentieth century. We are not historians happening to gather in church. We are pilgrims ourselves trying to create a new community of love on planet Earth, something more human than we have yet achieved. In Browne's words:

> In yellow meadows, I take no delight;
> Let me have those which are most red and white.

Sir Thomas synthesized religion, literature, and science. In his *Religio Medici* mercy and truth met together and reason and imagination kissed each other. Our international gathering is to stir in one pot science, religion and literature. This was Browne's historic role, not to keep disciplines in compartments but to allow each to fertilize the other. Those to whom we owe most in rediscovering Sir Thomas Browne – Sir Geoffrey Keynes, Professor Frank Livingstone-Huntley, Mrs Joan Bennett, Professor Basil Willey, and Professor Charles Raven – all wrote as men and women who cared about the integration of human knowledge and especially of religion, science and literature. They were all attracted to Browne because of his triple concern.

There can be no recovery of religion without a recovery of poetry and no survival for mankind without science, which is humane and disciplined and compassionate. Browne reminds us of the dazzling potentiality of the human mind when it opens itself to the best. 'Surely,' he says, 'there is a piece of divinity in us, something which was before the elements and owes no allegiance to the sun.' The piece of divinity we can only accept on faith. But it is no blind faith, but faith in the life of the spirit. He saw Christianity as a high water mark of humanism. 'Humanism', as R. H. Tawney said, 'is the antithesis not of Christianity but of materialism.'[2] Browne incarnated the wisdom of the old Hebrew preacher who taught long ago that 'a three-fold cord is not quickly broken' (Ecclesiastes 4.12).

How good that we are doing this in Norwich, for Browne, though he gained much from Winchester, Oxford, Montpellier, Padua and Leiden, believed in the genius of this place. I link him in my own mind with two great women in the city – Dame Julian and Edith Cavell. Julian declared, despite grim suffering and major tragedies, that 'All shall be well, and all shall be well, and all manner of thing shall be well,' because she believed, like Browne, that in every human personality there is a part which is untainted by evil. Edith Cavell, coming from a vicarage near here, founded scientific secular nursing in Belgium, met a tragic death during the First World War, and declared that 'I have seen death so often that it is not strange or fearful to me. . . . Standing as I do in view of God and eternity, I realize that patriotism is not enough. I must have no hatred or bitterness towards anyone.' Browne also refused to join the bitter religious and political hatreds of his day, though he remained a quiet Royalist. He had the reputation of remembering the names and personalities and characteristics of his patients. It matters that some doctors, like some parsons, should live in inner cities. Of course we must be magnanimous to others and ourselves, especially in old age when we forget names, like that old gentleman at a school reunion who said to a friend, 'Let me see, was it you or your brother who was killed in the war?' Today we honour someone who stayed in one place and really knew its people and its story, giving that high value to relationships we all laud in theory but find so hard in practice.

Mirror of his age

Edmund Gosse described Browne as a mirror of his age. When Browne looked at himself in the mirror he thanked God that he had escaped the sin of pride, and then proceeded, with entertaining naivety, to list his six languages and his knowledge of the names of all the constellations and most of the plants of the country. To read Browne must make everyone, now and then, long for gritty lucidity. One feels that in his mirror he saw very little agony, poignancy, or the struggles of the twice-born. He questioned received orthodoxy, such as the medieval symbolist's belief that nature is personal, and insisted on rigorous analysis. But there were blocks in his scientific objectivity: his pre-Copernican astronomy, his belief in witches, and the literal truth of the creation stories in Genesis. But still he insisted that tradition must be questioned and that human reason is competent to verify and falsify. He outlined a theology of trust – here we remember the teaching of Dame Cicely Saunders. We can trust human life to have a meaning. We can trust the universe to be on our side.

Look at the Browne monument here, in St Peter Mancroft Church, which describes his piety, integrity and learning.

His *piety* was a blend of prayer, worship and study. He was among those believers who reinterpreted God from the concept of the omnipotent king to the concept of the internal persuasive spirit – the crucial reinterpretation of the Renaissance and the Enlightenment. It was Browne, not Jung or Don Cupitt, who said, 'We carry within us the wonders we seek without us. There is all Africa and her prodigies in us.'

In his understanding of Christianity his science, poetry and faith interacted on each other. Some Christian traditionalists still think that 'scientific creationism' should be taught alongside evolutionary theories. I sense that Sir Thomas Browne's desire to hold scientific, poetic and religious truths together would lead him to agree with the philosopher-witness at the recent Arkansas trial who said that, 'If God exists, he cannot possibly want us to turn our backs on reason and sense, ostrich-like burrowing our heads in the comforting but arid sands of Genesis.'[3] Genesis is poetry and religion about 'Why', not exact science about 'How'.

His epitaph in this church next points to his *integrity* – finding out for ourselves, not leaving it to the book and to eyes other than our own. One of the delights of living in Norfolk is to sail out of the mud at Morston or down the narrow channel from Blakeney, along the coast towards Wells. Here you pass, in summer, great gatherings of seals. Here, too, you can see Blakeney Point, one of the largest meeting points for terns in all Europe. Browne inquired about a whale stranded on this piece of coast. It was typical of his determination to find out for himself, to do a dissection and not rely on the old authors. He shared that determined curiosity of Isaac Newton, Christopher Wren and the other members of the Royal

Society. But he had to make the most of East Anglia and rarely if ever visited London (though his son was a lecturer at the Barber-Surgeons). His own garden and house were a small botanic garden and domestic zoo. He dissected a dolphin and persuaded Lady Browne to dress and cook it and make an excellent savoury dish of it. Browne sent collars of it to the king's table after his return to Newmarket, which were 'well liked of'.

The king's recognition of Browne was the new age recognizing the old. R. W. Ketton-Cremer wrote, 'By 1671, Browne's opinions, as well as his style, were becoming somewhat out of date. New currents of thought, new discoveries and methods in medicine and chemistry were beginning to circulate. Science and reason were attaining a new standard of lucidity and order; and Browne, with his soaring and cloudy speculations, the stately eloquence and loaded splendour of his writing, his insurmountable belief in witchcraft and alchemy, belonged to the age which was passing.'[4] In Sir Geoffrey Keynes's gentler words, 'He is the great amphibian, the man torn between two worlds, ancient and modern, which he tried to reconcile with integrity.'

The third ascription in this church is *most learned*. His wisdom consisted not only in his accumulated information or his astonishing Baroque style but in the fusing of medicine, religion and literature. Listen to his goodbye in a colloquy with God. It is in the form of a prayer:

> The night is come like to the day,
> Depart not thou, Great God, away.
> Let not my sins, black as the night
> Eclipse the lustre of thy light.
> Keepe still in my horizon, for to me
> The Sunne makes not the day, but Thee.
> Thou whose nature cannot sleep
> On my temples sentry keep.
> Guard me 'gainst those watchful foes
> Whose eyes are open while mine close . . .

He ends his verses with these sentences: 'This is the dormitive I take to bedward; I need no other Laudanum than this to make me sleepe; after which I close my eyes in security, content to take my leave of the Sunne, and sleepe unto the Resurrection.'[5]

Heart of his faith

The heart of his faith lay in his prayers, his personal devotion. He prayed for his patients, for his family and especially for his son, Tom, and for himself. Prayer was, we might say, the helix in which his entwined concerns rose heavenwards.

Let me recall you to those windmills erected on the cartloads of bones of the past. If the dry bones of even the most attractive and intelligent commemoration are to live, then we must welcome the movement of the wind of the spirit. Only so can food be made for our minds and characters today. The message which Browne suggests is the need for binding together the insights of science, religion and literature. This is what he tried to do in this city 300 years ago. This is what we are called to do in our own cities round the world today, letting the spirit which comes from God move our minds a little further, so that we take a few more risks for the new life. We need a new passion for a new quality of life for everyone, and not leave this to our political leaders. Doctors, scientists, writers, all need to share in righting the wrongs of our time, the anxiety which grips us, the dark clouds of nuclear over-armament, racist intolerance, gross poverty in the Third World, and loneliness and materialism in our cities. We should all take risks for the new life, and risks which require us to go further in piety, in integrity and learning, to be reborn when we are old, standing not on our dignity but on our duty to devote ourselves to God and humanity.

Entertain the possibility of truth in religion. Let us agree that there are uncertainties, mysteries, doubts which go with us on our pilgrimage. These do not rule out concern with the immeasurables in religion and poetry. One day all mankind will trust, not to wealth, power and manipulation, but to the three-fold cord of science, religion and poetry. Let us each resolve to hasten that day.

Notes

1 G. Grigson, *The Faber Book of Epigrams and Epithets* (London: Faber, 1977), p. 8.
2 R. H. Tawney, *Equality* (London: Unwin Books, 1964), p. 85.
3 M. Ruse, 'A Philosopher at the Monkey Trial', *New Scientist*, 4 February 1982, pp. 317–19.

4 R. W. Ketton-Cremer, *Norfolk Portraits* (London: Faber and Faber, 1944), p. 15.
5 G. Keynes, 'Sir Thomas Browne', *British Medical Journal*, 1965 (2), pp. 1505–10.

Petra Clarke

Dr Petra Clarke, who died aged 69, represented London on the General Synod for ten years.

Trained as an obstetrician and gynaecologist, she had a career-long interest in public health aspects of nutrition; as a senior medical officer at the Department of Health, she drafted the official reports from the Committee on Medical Aspects of Food and Nutrition Policy, and commissioned three national studies of infant feeding, and a special study of the feeding of Asian infants in England.

In her work for the Church, she was active in, and for some years chaired, the London Movement for the Ordination of Women, and saw the final vote of more than two-thirds majorities in the Synod in 1992. She also spoke on this and on Christian Aid issues in other dioceses. In retirement, she worked for the UK charity, the Medical Foundation for the Care of Victims of Torture.

Her work as an examining doctor of victims arriving in London from around the world appears in *Rape as a Method of Torture*.[1] Her passionate professionalism allowed her to urge that even the raped refugees from Zimbabwe can be enabled to see that there is a future.

Born in Hertfordshire in 1938, to a Dutch mother and an English father, she was a caring, laughing and generous worker for peace, justice and human rights, with a powerful scientific knowledge of nutrition and human needs. She is remembered with gratitude especially at Holy Trinity, Tottenham, and by many patients and friends.

Note

1 Michael Peel (ed.), *Rape as a Method of Torture* (London: Medical Foundation for the Care of Victims of Torture, 2004).

Humanity should relish the precious mysteriousness of life

Twenty years ago Henry Moore was brought to St Paul's in a wheelchair to see the travertine marble *Mother and Child* he had designed for the cathedral. His hands could no longer carve but he had continued to draw. He was determined that the statue should be sympathetically positioned and well lit, and eventually he chose the aisle on the opposite side to John Donne, sculpted in his funeral shroud 300 years before. Moore gazed intently at his figures – the baby half-hidden within its mother – and said in his faintly York-shire accent: 'It's a great mystery, a great mystery.' No one there liked to ask him which mystery he meant – the artist's creativity, the coming of Christ or the presence of the Spirit.

Perhaps Moore was thinking of the mysteriousness of birth and life itself. His first, controversial *Mother and Child*, for St Matthew's, Northampton, had been carved in 1943 when his experiences as a war artist were vivid. He had just drawn the sleeping bodies of the troglodyte shelterers in the London Underground, as well as the miners in his father's old colliery near Castleford. He longed to affirm the human body and the mysterious life within it, especially when threatened by indiscriminate bombing or the harsh demands of coal mining. He had almost been killed himself at the battle of Cambrai in the First World War.

His last *Mother and Child* at St Paul's is his plea to humanity to recognize the precious mysteriousness of life, and to reverence, not destroy itself. He was determined to affirm humanity's often missed mysterious splendour. His *Mother and Child* expresses a protective tenderness, so that this statue in London's cathedral is a public proclamation about love for children in the city that had experienced the chimney boys and was to be shaken by the tragedy of Victoria Climbié.

For others, nature has been the medium that reveals the mysteriousness around us. John Constable, no doubt thinking of Flatford Mill, wrote: 'The sound of water escaping from mill-dams etc, willows, old rotten planks, slimy posts and brickwork, I love such things.' He wanted his paintings to be full 'of religious and moral feeling', showing 'how much of His nature God has implanted in the mind of man'. Constable, like Wordsworth, believed that there is a mysterious wonder in the natural world, perhaps especially in his clouds. Sir Thomas Browne put these feelings in a sentence: 'I lose myself in a mystery.' Certainly Moore and Constable felt that pointing to the mystery did not conflict with their work in stone and paint.

Wise educationists remember our need to be alert to mystery. Today there is a field centre near Flatford where children from junior schools all over the country can stay for two or three days and nights to put on their wellies and view the night sky and the stars' reflection in the water. Pond dipping, seeing and naming the Pleiades for the first time, and the surprises and fun of night walks remain fixed in their minds as fascinating memories. They experience mystery.

Today London children are guided round St Paul's by teachers and volunteers and can feel the wonder of the Mother and the emerging Child of Moore's imagination. They may wonder about their own birth and the birth of Jesus. The statue is darkened by their fingertips but Moore hoped that would happen and had no fear of damage. 'We could make another,' he said with a smile, as though to discover wonder was worth a risk. Both at Flatford and at St Paul's some may experience a sense of a divine plan in which we ourselves and Jesus Christ's life, teaching, and risen spirit all have a place.

When the British Graham Land expedition set off in 1934 for three years among the ice, their geologist and chaplain Launcelot Fleming took with them a prayer written by a Cambridge college principal: 'Almighty Father, ruler of the elements and maker of the universe in its tremendous majesty . . . Grant us a fuller realisation of the wonder of Thy presence, which is in all and through all.' Today, when science is guiding humanity more than ever before, the path forward in religion will be through wonder as well as through texts; more through trying to meet Christ's tough demands than from codifying earlier moral customs.

The ancient texts, Sinai and the Psalms and the Gospels, speak much of wonder. The artists and painters, the children and the explorers also affirm the many-splendoured things. God is a God of wonder, vulnerability and gentle tenderness, not to be muffled or tamed.

Ancient religious texts can help us on our way but not if we hope to become, to use a term coined by the former Bishop of Durham, 'certainty-wallahs'. Rather we should expect mysteries beyond precise words. To quote Launcelot Fleming: 'We are groping for a religion in which we can believe without evasion, without dishonest ambiguities, without self-deception, without superstition. The Christian religion began with friendship. We shall never find it in isolated searching.'

Fleming the scientist and believer seemed, to some of those who heard him, to be saying, with extreme modesty: 'I don't see much myself but these are the lines along which I am sure we ought to look if we are to find a way into the mystery of God . . . Our Lord's way of teaching was always from the known to the unknown, from the human to the divine, from the natural to the supernatural. With astonishing consistency he practised what he preached.'

Charles Groves

In his passport, the conductor Charles Groves described himself as 'Musician'. If his passport had gone on to state where he was born as a musician, he would surely have said 'St Paul's Cathedral'. How fitting then that his funeral should be here in the Cathedral Crypt, this womb of faith.

We are here beside his family, who are much in our thoughts and prayers, his beloved Hilary, their children Sally and Mary and Jonathan, and his seven grandchildren. It was so clear at the baptism of Tamara, one of the grandchildren, in this chapel eight years ago, how proud he was of you all. So, as he wished, we meet together to say farewell – family, friends, musicians and admirers. Charles's ashes will be taken to the Church of St Levan in Cornwall, where every Sunday he and Hilary used to join the whole community in worship.

Charles was an only child, orphaned; his father never recovered from the trenches of World War I and his mother died when he was ten. He came to St Paul's Choir School in the mid-1920s when things were rather dark. One of his jokes was that the 40 boys had to share one towel and that all sorts of creatures scurried around in the cellars. Certainly for much of his time the dome was boarded up, the eight pillars which support it insecure. Sheffield steel chains were inserted with difficulty – the work which in fact saved the dome from collapse in World War II. Charles was the head chorister in the service which marked the reopening of the re-constructed dome – a truly triumphant occasion.

Through all the years which followed, despite very demanding musical tasks, and a quite unusual devotion to the hard work of supporting musical education and young musicians, Charles came back again and again to this cathedral. It was his parish church; he always talked with other regulars. He would sit in the stalls and was a source of sanity and encouragement – qualities much needed in cathedrals. In the 1980s he joined the Court of Advisors and said he was proud to be a member, together with representative London lay men and lay women, the Governor of the Bank of England, the Director of the GLC, Lady Elspeth Howe – who heads the new Cathedrals Commission – and a number of others; he would consider with them the mission of the cathedral in the contem-porary world and was always able to look and to plan ahead. He also devoted himself to the re-endowment of the music of the cathedral. All the time one felt that it was his home and he shared responsibility for its being a place of warmth and friendliness and inspiration. He had time to listen and to think, to laugh and to advise – and you felt that in the background there was a true con-cern for everyone; he always spoke in discussion as an experienced, unpretentious, wise and caring musician.

Perhaps to go a little deeper into Charles's personality, we need to turn to the poets, to those who write the songs. None is older, more dramatic, more mysterious or more difficult to translate than the song of Deborah, where we are told to 'Sing in the places of drawing water where they rehearse the righteous acts of the Lord' (Judges 5.11). For Charles, churches were watering places, fresh springs, not difficult buildings where a careful, correct code must always be followed. He liked concerts in churches and disagreed with Adrian Boult, who discouraged clapping at the end of a concert. Charles loved doing music in churches and cathedrals. He said with his customary generous twinkle of Adrian Boult, 'Give him time, he'll come round in the end.' Because Charles felt at home in church, and could speak with integrity and sincerity of the righteous acts of the Lord, he saw churches as places where we could sing and rehearse. He saw churches as places about reality, not about convention; as places of creativity, not of clinical repetition. Just as at Bournemouth, of all places, he had defied tradition and sold raffle tickets in the streets, and in 1974 at the Last Night of the Proms had made in fact a political speech, so he was liberated in his work in churches. Here, he believed, we can rehearse the righteous acts of the Lord and here we can find places where water is drawn, where there are fresh springs for our parched personalities.

Hundreds upon hundreds have felt this truth about Charles and have written to his family to express their admiration and sorrow. Perhaps we should imagine in our thoughts and prayers the whole cathedral above us, every seat filled with someone who has gained from the work of Charles Groves. He loved large-scale occasions, especially at Liverpool Cathedral, and people sensed this. But he liked to think of himself as a GP, not as a consultant. Certainly the number of those who have written shows how extraordinarily he met the individual needs of those who listened. In these large-scale occasions – Mahler symphonies, the Berlioz *Grande Messe des Morts* and many more – his integrity and skill gripped individual listeners who felt that something beyond them, some hidden spring, was being opened through the conductor's personality – just for them – one by one.

And so we say farewell and Godspeed and thanksgiving, especially here, that Charles continued to find the Church of God a watering place where he could rehearse with integrity the righteous acts of the Lord. How characteristic that someone who spent much time on the podium and received so much applause in so many of the world's cities should wish us to say goodbye in a crypt, rather hidden, rather private. Talking with Charles, you always felt that there were hidden truths, mysteries we shall not quite fathom, clouds of unknowing which cannot be described but where we sense that only love can take us further. Reverence and integrity went with vulnerability and a feeling that not everything can be described. Charles seemed to say that life was not a matter of correct codes or careful creeds, it was a matter of being prepared to sing in the places where they draw water and rehearse again and again the righteous acts of the Lord.

Tom Baker

Tom Baker was an ordained scholar who spent many years in a succession of posts training clergy for the ministry of the Church of England.

He was acutely aware of the need to be able to serve with integrity in a secular society, where often the old words no longer resonated. As he told the General Synod in a famous speech:

> The fact is that some convinced Christians do not find it at all easy either to grasp or communicate the reality of God in today's society. Although they have no doubt that they believe in Him, somehow He seems to have withdrawn from the scene and the traditional language no longer seems quite to work as it used to.

In parishes, theological colleges, at cathedrals and as a preacher, author and reviewer, Baker addressed this ultimate question for today's churches.

Baker was born at Southampton in 1920. He won a scholarship from King Edward VI School to Exeter College, Oxford, where he gained a First in Theology, and was ordained in 1944 to King's Heath, Birmingham. After three years as a curate he was sent by the Bishop, E. W. Barnes, to an Anglo-Catholic church without much congregation, on the understanding that if it could not be regenerated it would be amalgamated. Baker survived this challenge, as usual making the best of difficulties, won the affection of the parish, and the numbers increased. After nine years, aided by his mother, aunt and grandmother, who turned the vicarage into a happy home for him and the parish, he was moved to become Sub-Warden and New Testament lecturer at Lincoln Theological College.

Lincoln had already gained a tradition of disciplined spirituality and radical theological thinking. Baker's learning, clarity and hard work, combined with his humour, parochial experience, musical gifts and human warmth, made him a shrewd but tolerant guide. Students who believed that everything they had been taught about the scriptures and the creeds by their favourite vicar in the past was literally true, were introduced to a new and sometimes painful freedom of thought.

Geoffrey Fisher, the Archbishop of Canterbury, tried hard to recruit Baker from Lincoln to be his principal chaplain at Lambeth but Baker was as always without ambition (and perhaps a little shy) so, as a friend put it, the Archbishop's 'almost irresistible force met a quite immovable object'. Instead, in 1960 Baker began his 11 creative years as Principal of Wells Theological College.

As at Lincoln, he insisted that theology can only be studied within its social and cultural context. Some found that being introduced to the demythologizing work of Rudolf Bultmann was disturbing, but by a careful use of a seminar system, and by listening, questioning and worshipping in small groups, the difficulties were faced with integrity. There was basic reading for everyone but highly selective reading as well for each member of the college. There was no large institutional building; instead the students lived in groups of five or six in Vicar's Close. They learned to share each other's jokes and problems.

Training in worship was greatly assisted by the use of the beautiful Wells Cathedral crypt with furniture largely made by the students themselves. Worship was in the round and high standards were required in combining the traditional with the innovative. Visits to study and share French worship, both Catholic and at Taizé, were valuable. Links with Wesley College, Bristol were designed in part to use the resources of Bristol University, where Baker taught part time, and with the hope of uniting the two colleges as Anglicans and Methodists came together.

Unfortunately, as student numbers declined in all the churches, the hierarchy decided to close Wells and move it to Salisbury, where eventually both the teacher training college and the theological college were themselves closed. It was a sad end to the experiments which were prophetic for the Church at the end of the century.

After three years as Archdeacon of Bath, where his common sense and efficiency were appreciated, he was appointed Dean of Worcester and for 11 years Baker was one of the foremost Three Choirs' Festival deans. As a skilled and well-qualified pianist with a natural generosity of spirit he got on well with the musical establishments at Worcester, which were intrigued by the catholicity of his musical tastes. At a famous cathedral party they sang his praises:

> He loves all kinds of music,
> From opera to pop,
> He can't abide poor Wesley,
> It makes his spirits drop.
> He quite likes C. V. Stanford,
> He loves a Gershwin tune,
> And if you play him Wagner,
> He fades into a swoon.

Baker published both on biblical studies, *What is the New Testament?* (1969), and on the worship of the Christian community, *Questioning Worship* (1977), and received from his friends a book of essays, *The Reality of God* (1986). These all argued for a reassessment of what is often preached and taught in the parishes.

Baker emphasized the speed of change in the thinking of churchgoers. He faced some loss of enjoyment in worship and a decline in churchgoing. Instead he saw the Christian community as an open, humble movement springing from 'the things concerning Jesus, drawing on the rich literary, artistic and musical traditions of the past and living today for the generous transformation of human life'. He taught a deft use of language in church, avoiding religiosity and unafraid of modernity, critical scholarship or scientific thinking.

Few deans were so entertaining or surprising. Colleagues in the chapter were wrenched out of their settled ways to see films, to plunge into Iris Murdoch or listen to Wagner. Some found playing four-hand piano duets at high speed unforgettable, or enjoyed visiting France with him. The influence of Continental scholarship and thinking was deep within him, giving a depth to the way he understood faith.

His influence was extended by his visits to theological colleges as a chief inspector, his acute reviews of New Testament studies and his speeches at the General Synod. It was sad that during his time at Worcester he suffered a period of intense grief and loneliness at the deaths of his mother and his aunt, and owing to a severe throat illness was for years unable to speak in public. But his goodness, absence of cant, and questioning mind still exerted their attraction. In retirement at the Charterhouse his diary was rarely empty.

Theme 6

CHILDREN AND YOUNG PEOPLE

A book which celebrates achievement inevitably has a backward-looking element. This section begins by describing and assessing successes already achieved in supporting young people, especially through education. It also looks forward to the future, symbolized by today's children and young people. It considers their ways of moving towards faith, which may not be along traditionally accepted lines.

God backs the poor

It is a sad quirk of history that the life and deeds of Richard Oastler (1788–1861), a powerful Christian critic of the Industrial Revolution's cruelties to children, have been largely ignored by the Church of England. Less culpably, perhaps, he has been ignored by Methodists too – although John Wesley blessed the infant Oastler during his last visit to Yorkshire.

Oastler insisted that while the political world was devoted to the Reform Bill and the religious world to evangelism, Tractarianism and the abolition of slavery, the tragic lives of children working more than 19 hours a day in the mills should not be forgotten. He wrote to Edward Venables Vernon Harcourt, Archbishop of York: 'The factory question is, my Lord, a soul question; it is souls against the pounds, shillings and pence.' The archbishop made no reply.

When a young girl, arriving late at the mill gates to start her 14-hour shift, was strapped by an attendant, Oastler held a meeting of hundreds at Huddersfield to protest and brought a large leather strap crashing down on the platform to arouse the conscience of the crowd.

Many politicians protested against such religious criticism. Palmerston argued that to legislate for working hours was 'vicious and wrong in principle'. The children had to wait for 40 years until a radical Tory government under Disraeli passed an effective Factory Act that compelled magistrates to protect children from the worst abuses of the Industrial Revolution. By this time Oastler had spent three years in prison for threatening to incite children to push their grandmothers' knitting needles into the spinning machinery.

During his years in London prisons (1841–4) his weekly *Fleet Papers* (written in the Fleet Prison) became famous. Each copy was headed with the motto: 'The Altar, the Throne and the Cottage'. He publicized the harsh elements of the industrial system, and printed a series of verdicts by Petty Sessions in South Wiltshire to illustrate how magistrates penalized farm labourers. He published hymns on the sufferings of factory children.

The Fleet Papers, widely distributed, were filled with examples of injustices in the system from all over England. My own set of copies went first from London to a pharmacist in Sunderland, and from there were forwarded to a fell parson in Cumberland. They sound an apocalyptic note: 'These are not common times – our institutions have been shaken, the rights of the poor have been violated.' He wrote of the 'horrible system of selling agricultural labourers and their families to the mill owners': 'All our manufacturing towns have become military stations – they are garrisoned to protect an antisocial power against an industrious, loyal people!' On his release *The Times* carried a leading article entitled 'The ransomed patriot'. It claimed: 'Mr Oastler is the providential organ of the oppressed and suffering poor. Those who do not see and know and feel what he does are not competent judges.'

Returning in triumph to Yorkshire, he was met by hundreds of factory children carrying small white flags inscribed with the jingle:

> The King is released, the captive is free,
> Long may he live, and blessed may he be.

They marched from Brighouse to Huddersfield and bands played to crowds of several thousand. It mattered to the whole northern community that a respectable, established citizen, notable for arguing for the abolition of slavery abroad, should back humanity for children at home. Country people, accustomed to the charities of rural parishes, had moved north to the factories where they found no parish relief, only workhouses where husband and wife were often separated.

Oastler was an orator and a prophet who insisted that Christianity was relevant to industrial society. Tall and broad-shouldered, he was sure that the Bible was on the side of the poor. A nineteenth-century Amos, he believed that policy ought to be made 'not according to the market, but by estimating God's intention to create a caring, compassionate human community'.

He protested against Malthus's pessimistic population doctrines. He denounced some of the bishops as believers in a doctrine of devils to produce a legal code of atrocious laws 'at variance with every precept of our holy religion'. He recruited a few MPs and the Scottish reformer Dr Thomas Chalmers in his campaign to restore Britain's social conscience.

Oastler made a sustained attack on the injustice of the establishment. 'If the Church, the Throne and the aristocracy are determined to rob the poor man of his liberty, of his wife and of his children, then is the Church no longer that of Christ – the Throne no longer that of England – then are the nobles no longer safeguards of the people . . . Then with their bitterest foes would I cry "Down with them, down with them all to the ground".' Oastler's courage helped to save England from revolution in the hungry 1840s.

Today the protests about worldwide hunger from Christian Aid, Tearfund and Cafod. Are sometimes criticized for being 'political' and 'not religious'. But the prophetic within religion, so desperately needed during the Industrial Revolution, remains as vital in our days of disaster and famine.

Choice for changing faith

My 11-year-old grandson, leading me on a dark winter night to Headington Quarry Church in Oxford, where he was to be confirmed, asked: 'What about the Crusades?' Having no time to discuss the motives of St Bernard or the villainous sacking of Constantinople, I said: 'They were bad.' Satisfied, he led me on into the church, which was warm, welcoming and packed with people: the 15 candidates and five adults, who were also to be baptized.

It was a special scene reflecting its Narnia window commemorating C. S. Lewis, who came to this church after he was converted by J. R. R. Tolkien, the author of *The Lord of the Rings* and imaginative creator of the evil Orcs and of the Hobbits' struggle to rid Middle Earth of terror. Tolkien and Lewis were convinced that the Christian myth is a true myth. In Lewis's words, 'Sometimes fairy stories may say best what's to be said.'

At the baptisms the bishop sloshed the water around, assuring us that the water stood for the love of God pouring over us all. The baptisms, confirmations, first communions and the party in the village hall afterwards were hints of a new world we have yet to realize. We prayed that God would give us power to live a new life in the dark world outside – a naive prayer, perhaps, but has innocence no power?

In today's England, many inside and outside the churches reconsider the question of faith. Last year Nick Doughty, a Reuters correspondent who covered the fighting in Kosovo, and father of a young family, was struck by cancer. In the months before his death he wrote an apologia to be read at his funeral, explaining his unexpected decision to affirm faith and be confirmed. Lying on a couch at home in North London, he was too ill to go to a church, so after much thought and many conversations with Claire Robson, his vicar, he was confirmed at home by a retired missionary archbishop.

In Doughty's own words:

> After my diagnosis and a few weeks stumbling through tears and rage and fear and confusion, I started to take walks in the City, anything to get away from the turmoil inside. One of these walks took me on a Sunday ... towards St Paul's Cathedral. I went inside, my

mood one of grim challenge. 'OK God, if you're real, if you mean anything, show me now if you're there, now is the time. Show me . . .' No, the scales did not fall from my eyes . . . something much greater happened. A profound sense of peace flooded through me in that great church. Someone was with me, someone who felt my anguish and torment very deeply . . .

Statistics suggest that in the Church of England between 30,000 and 40,000 people are confirmed each year, young and not so young. Many young people are 'collectors' – often of varieties of cards. For two months before his confirmation I sent a weekly picture to my grandson which he collected and called 'Confirmation Cards', including the standing Stenness Stones as a reminder that there was faith and religion before Abraham; St Paul's among the flames in December 1940 saved by volunteers, as a hint that we have to be brave and back what is good; and two prayers to learn by heart – 'God be in my head' and 'Lighten our darkness' – and a selection of others.

The vicar's sessions mattered in these months. This 11-year-old raised the question of Gene Robinson, the Bishop of New Hampshire: 'What did you decide about him?' I asked. 'I said I needed time to think it out,' he replied. Would that 'thinking it out' could become normal for both young and old. When Tolkien and Lewis affirmed that Christianity is a true myth, they left open the question: which parts are true literal history and which are not true science and not true history?

Today is a time for considered change in religious faith. 'In a higher world, it is otherwise,' wrote John Henry Newman, 'but here below, to live is to change, and to be perfect is to have changed often.' Moments of choice, one-to-one occasions for dialogue provided by churches and religious groups and discussions in schools after ethical, philosophical and religious lessons are seminal for the vernalization of the spirit of freedom in the mind of the young.

In the contemporary words of John Wilkins, a distinguished Roman Catholic journalist: 'Young Christians in the Europe of today come to their faith through individual choice . . . they have a thirst for religious experience and good teaching.' Those who are searching in many denominations and religions are reconsidering those Gospel words: 'When the Spirit of truth comes, he will reveal to you the things to come' (John 16.12).

The search for meaning is at the top of the agenda for many of the next generation and for others facing crisis.

Why the kids are all right

This summer Alec, a New York boy, stood at the top of the stairs that lead to the crypt of St Paul's with his mother and his younger sister and said, rather loudly: 'I want to see Lawrence of Arabia.' Fortunately, he was heard by a Sister, who took him right through the crypt to Eric Kennington's head of Lawrence. Alec danced for joy, skipping and smiling among the tombs of Nelson and Wellington. How Lawrence would have relished the scene – Lawrence, who enjoyed meetings of opposites, famously describing King Faisal, worn, a face like a dagger, meeting Allenby, gigantic and red and merry. Alec wanted to find adventure in St Paul's and his happiness at Lawrence's memorial was his worship.

When I was a little older than Alec, the most compelling place in my home cathedral at Chester was the memorial to Jack Cornwell. He was shown standing in the open on the deck of HMS *Chester* at Jutland. The inscription told of his fidelity when he received the shrapnel wounds from which he died three days later in hospital at Grimsby. He was only 16 and was awarded posthumously the Victoria Cross and nationally commemorated by the Scout movement, of which he was an enthusiastic member in his parish of Little Ilford, Manor Park. He mattered because he was 16 and lived in my century.

A Roman Catholic youth leader insisted that anyone still practising his or her Christianity into their mid-teens in our secular society is in need of temporary communities in which they feel safe talking about their faith and facing tasks together requiring skill and determination.

In July 1984, the south transept of York Minster was swept by flames, destroying the roof and the medieval wooden vault beneath. Robert Aagaard, a Yorkshire conservator, gathered 25 members of young people's Cathedral Camps, housed them in the empty deanery and got them up to the north transept, dangerously full of rubbish, including newspapers of the previous century. A farming engineer from North Yorkshire in his early twenties put safety roping round the high clerestory pillars and more than 150 sacks of pigeon droppings as well as flammable debris were carried down a hundred feet of steep steps. All the young members of the party grew in admiration and respect for the minster and its spiritual task today and in the future.

The minster's staff were courageous and realistic enough to accept the help and the questions of the young campers, who now have lifelong experience of the vision of the original builders and the hopes of today's Church.

Many young people experience opportunities to care for the disadvantaged through their schools, Oxfam, CIIR and Christian Aid. Parishes are mounting costly and complicated projects to enable teenagers to travel and to work for justice. In Rustington in West Sussex teenage members of the Wayfarers, a joint Methodist and Anglican youth group, financed themselves by fund-raising and donations, and travelled to Kenya to give voluntary help in an African school for street children.

Fourteen-year-old Jessica went with some trepidation, daunted at the prospect of acting as a teaching assistant. Because of a shortage of teachers she found herself actually teaching a class of about 35 children with minimal supervision. An 18-year-old, anxious about possible terrorist activity in Kenya, returned home moved and humbled by the experience. The visit was so successful that Carol, the Wayfarers' leader, was asked to take the group again this year, as friendships flourished and grew.

More confident now in their roles as classroom assistants, some have begun to learn Swahili. This group of young Christians have overcome their fears, and learnt to face the poverty they saw – which contrasted sharply with the friendly openness and willingness to share of the Kenyan children. One of the youngsters commented, 'I learnt more in two weeks in Kenya than I could in six months in England.'

Parishes and cathedrals can be places of initiative for a fair, caring and just life for all humanity. The message of William Temple can be heard again. The Bible given to me 60 years ago when priested in Sheffield by a friend of Temple, emphasized the New Testament words: 'God has not given to us the spirit of fear, but of power and love and discipline.'

The church in the factory area where I served was destroyed in the Blitz, the church where I first celebrated Communion soon rightly became a Muslim centre for part of a Pakistani community. In this challenging environment, teenagers could be spiritually positive, encouraging a lay youth worker, undermined by three years in a Japanese PoW camp, and building up his self-confidence by their humour and acceptance.

Our spirituality needs to recognize this longing in the younger generation to join in the demanding struggle for world fairness and justice and mutual caring.

High ideals for the next generation

George Herbert, the poet and priest, urged his contemporaries to 'pitch thy behaviour low and thy projects high; so shalt thou humble and magnanimous be'. He was writing just before the Civil War, his century's form of terrorism.

Two of those in succeeding centuries, Thomas Coram (1688–1751), a shipbuilder and merchant, and Thomas Barnardo (1845–1905), a student at the London Hospital, accepted as their eventual vocation the welfare of children. They wore themselves out and used every means available in their culture to create projects high enough to heed Jesus' grim prophecy that a millstone would be fastened round the necks of those who harm the generation that follows them. Coram and Barnardo eventually gave up other projects, shipbuilding in Massachusetts and being a missionary to China, for their children-centred London institutions.

The work carried on under their names is alive in imaginative forms today. The Coram Family has launched a survival pack scheme for young men and women leaving care or prison. Barnardo's is raising £1 million for its work with children who have been sexually exploited. A 13-year-old whose 'boyfriend' posted indecent photographs of her on the Internet wrote: 'It started off as a bit of fun – I thought he loved me.'

Coram and Barnardo's are in touch with more than 100,000 children and Barnardo's employ a staff of 6,000. The high inspiration which came centuries ago to the founders is now the spirit alive in a new generation of carers.

Hogarth gave Coram some of his paintings; Handel, his fair copy of *Messiah*; and the foundation still possesses them. Today musicians and artists often support child care.

In September 1905 London was magnanimous at the funeral of Thomas Barnardo. With hindsight he had not always been right: he never qualified as a doctor but used the title to aid the children's cause. He was often autocratic, perhaps because he had been bullied at school. He avoided committees and accountants until several bankruptcies and court cases forced him to accept them. Today we would question sending children to families in Canada and using dubious 'Before' and 'After' photographs. But Edwardian England gave him a spectacular goodbye – a lying in state at the pub he had converted into a coffee house and a procession through streets filled with mourners from Limehouse to Liverpool Street. Best of all his debts were paid off and Barnardo's has continued to grow for the following century. Perhaps he would have been proudest of all about the pressure it and other organizations brought upon Westminster until finally last year Parliament appointed a Commissioner for Children for England. At 60 he had been worn out by work but his aim that no child should be turned away had been accepted by the nation.

There has been a massive effort by many children's organizations working at home and abroad this year. Here is an arena where the words of Jesus about the antagonisms and power struggles between generations (Mark 13.12) are experienced and, it is hoped, resolved. In 1968 the students at the Sorbonne proclaimed how they longed for freedom to be themselves and think for themselves. 'Plus de maîtres, Plus de maîtres', they scribbled on the walls.

Mike, a boy in the care of Coram, put in homelier terms the constrictions of neglect and lack of love: 'I don't have happy memories of childhood. My mum drank all the time and could not cope with having a kid. I never even met my dad ... My story may not sound anything really great.'

Like the Sorbonne students he is asking for freedom which is denied by parents who do not put children first or by movements which simply call for more prisons. When George Herbert mentioned 'behaviour low' he was asking for quiet hard work and consistent love in child care. There is a need for forgiveness between generations in families and in the state. It is too easy to spot the eccentricities of Coram and Barnardo in a Lytton Strachey-style biography and miss the height of the aims of the child philanthropists.

This year many events are designed to enable a sharing of their vision of justice and love for all children. There are celebrations – corporate, business community and sporting – as well as events in churches from St Giles, Edinburgh to King's College, Cambridge. These are all invitations to realize the imaginative magnanimity of child care as proclaimed in the Psalms and the Gospels: 'Thou hast brought praise to perfection from the mouths of babes and sucklings' (Matthew 21.16). On this ancient vision realized century after century depends the peace of humankind.

EPILOGUE:
HOPE FOR THE FUTURE

These three short essays sum up the book's message that God is at work in the world today through the lives of men and women and that this work, built on the firm foundations of the past, will open new and exciting prospects yet to come.

The journey towards understanding

Sauntering in summer on a Saturday evening in the Highlands, we arrived unbooked at Inchnadamph.

Could they put us up for the night? Yes, they had two empty rooms. Would we prefer one with a key but no view, or one with a view but no key? Like most holiday-makers, I imagine, we chose the room with a view and were rewarded next day by seeing the deer down in the glen and the sunrise gleaming on Loch Assynt. The door had to be kept unlocked because it was the fire escape for that floor of the hotel.

Religion encourages us to go for a view, to have faith that there is a meaning to the journey of life and its relationships and that, for all the value of a settled home, we are pilgrims who should travel lighter than we find comfortable. John Bunyan's *Pilgrim's Progress* is, he tells us, a journey from this world to that which is to come; but the light of the celestial city is experienced during the journey and not only at the end.

Light seemed to shine inside Pilgrim even in Doubting Castle when only his companion Hopeful could rescue him from imprisoning depression. More recently W. H. Auden's three wise men said: 'To discover how to be human now is the reason we follow this star.'

It cheers to think of life as a journey towards understanding. I was encouraged that Lady Donaldson, the first woman to be Lord Mayor of London, chose *The Pilgrim's Progress* as her gift from St Paul's as she faced a challenging year. We all need time to attend to our journey. Visitors to London down the centuries are well advised to heed Wren's epitaph: *Si monumentum requiris, circumspice.*

Some of those who walk the Pennine Way or the road to Compostela, especially if they are walking alone, say that just putting one foot after another disciplines the mind in meditation.

Sauntering while sailing has special joys. In late summer Hickling, one of the largest of the Norfolk Broads, possesses an almost tangible solitariness. What you see was seen by Cotman and Crome, unchanged for centuries. The shallow water laps on the boat. Swallow-tailed butterflies still flutter on Candle Dyke. Terns still make their vertical dives, and warblers chase from reed to reed. Clouds drift across the sky out to the nearby sea. The skies are so immense; they speak of the spirit's universality. The contrast with our self-tormented world and in-turned institutions, even religious institutions, stresses the divine plea that we should grow in human understanding and compassionate maturity. The tendency of churches to criticize, even sometimes bully, each other seems rebuked by such vast, open skies.

Sauntering gives us time to reflect on futures that never came, life ending in abrupt tragedy. Nowhere is this more gently expressed than in a 1771 inscription in the tiny fellside chapel of Cartmell Fell, one of the hidden holy places of the north. The lettering is elegant, the stone half-concealed in the chancel – you would miss it unless you were really attending:

> Underneath this stone a mould'ring Virgin lies,
> Who was the pleasure once of Human Eyes.
> Her Blaze of Charms Virtue well approv'd;
> The Gay admired her, much the parents lov'd.
> Transitory life! Death untimely came.
> Adieu, farewell, I only leave my name.

Betty Poole was a little girl who died aged three. Those who mourn the children of Soham or those dying this year in the starving deserts of Sudan will echo those grieving words on the fragility of the young. Summer can give us the moments we need to pause, reflect, mourn and give thanks.

Everyday resurrections

Our culture is ambiguous about Easter, the proclamation that life can triumph over death. The aching shock of caring for a relative with an incurable disease and then the death of the beloved does not fit an annual holiday season. It feels more like being plunged into a rock-strewn whirlpool. But a friend said after the death of her husband: 'Yes, I experience moments of resurrection,' thinking of shining moments for him and for her in the past and now. Colleagues remembered a private incident in the courts – he was a lawyer – when he felt that the widow of a fatal accident victim was meanly compensated. He not only waived his fee but also made a payment from his own pocket to make up what he considered a fair award. Though he would have been the last to say it, it felt as though eternity had broken into routine for an instant.

Several of the stories read at Easter have similar hints of recognizing resurrection not as a steady state but momentary, more like flashing lights than somewhere on a map. Death does irreparably change relationships. To recognize Christ as risen was beyond the two disciples walking to Emmaus. It was beyond common sense and required a change in direction of life and a subversion of earlier attitudes.

British communities after the two world wars, confronting collective grief and hidden anger at the casualties, wished to express something they sensed in the fallen. In the Cheshire village of Wrenbury, 26 were killed in 1914–18, and eight in 1939–45. The church, the councillors, the British Legion and local activists worked for a better life in the community – new council housing instead of tied agricultural workers' cottages; mains water and electricity. They elected a sandstone cross in the churchyard with the names of the dead and added a simple inscription from the Greek tradition: 'The burial place of noble men is in the hearts of their friends'. Easter is the enemy of the status quo.

Janet Morley, a leading contemporary liturgist, in *Bread of Tomorrow: Praying with the World's Poor* (SPCK/Christian Aid), notes the bemused difficulty of recognition in the Gospel Easter stories and wonders whether we, as the relatively wealthy of the world, find Easter elusive because we are so far from the hungry poor. She gives us 22 prayers from around the world which recognize resurrection. Those oppressed by war, Aids, civil strife and starvation can be the concern of our national policies, charitable cash and prayers. We can roll back the stone of indifference and have a moment of hope.

Most English liturgies, ancient or modern, lack the language which can inspire our concern for street children, the impoverished or victims of sex tourism. It is no accident that the Gospel resurrection stories were about recognizing new relationships with travellers, fishermen, sceptics and the crowds. Morley quotes a prayer from Guatemala entitled 'Threatened with Resurrection', praying for 'the old man without a doctor, asking for the bread of justice at the door of a locked church'. A recent immigrant, a victim of torture, achieved an English allotment. It was fresh life, resurrection life, to be able to grow food for his family in safety. Our current orthodoxies, scientific materialism or literal interpretation of what happened to Christ's body, may block our recognition of the flashes of resurrection which come our way from God.

The Bible asks: 'Can these dry bones live?' An honest answer, especially in our embittered world, seems to be: 'Impossible'. But the mystical writer Monica Furlong, who died in the past year, replied: 'Impossibility leads straight to the heart of passion, the passion of man, the passion of God'. We have all had moments when in deep suffering light dawns, reconciliation, newness and creativity take control and hope rises again. If we have experienced in this life the miracle of gracious freshness – as individuals, as churches, as countries – is it impossible that after death we may be given moments of resurrection? We do well to pray those Old and New Testament words: 'Old things are passed away; behold all things are become new.'

Love is at the heart of human life

Critics of the New Year festivities sometimes describe the thankfulness and hope and resolutions of this time as hypocrisy in our times of terrorism, threats and unpredictable disasters. But the tensions of modern life need not inhibit altruistic action. Sometimes this is expressed through the writing of letters.

A small group of Amnesty International supporters in the London suburb of Merton have been so horrified by the sentence of stoning on the young Nigerian mother who gave birth to her daughter outside marriage that they organized more than one and a third million supporters of a letter of protest. The court has now ruled that she be exempted from stoning until her baby is weaned, and central authorities may intervene in the cause of mercy.

The Merton petitioners continue to press for amnesty and carried a painting of Amina, the mother, with her tiny baby Wasila, to the Nigerian Embassy. One of the petitioners wrote a poem with the questioning words 'Who among you will cast the first stone?', that crucial question the Babe of Bethlehem grew up to ask. Terrorists' threats to London's way of life have not inhibited people in their search for justice. Some of the most moving paintings of the events at Bethlehem include the mothers with the Innocents hideously murdered after the Nativity, as if to plead that Christmas stay alive in a world that includes psychopathic killers.

It is not hypocritical to show thankfulness and resolution in the troughs of life. When Oscar Wilde was released from two years' imprisonment, mainly in Reading Gaol, he fled to France both to change his name and to escape British criticism of homosexuals. In his first week of freedom he wrote a startling letter of thanks to Major James Nelson, the governor of Reading Gaol. He expressed his 'affectionate gratitude to you for the real care you took of me at the time when I was mentally upset . . . When one knows the strong joy of gratitude to God and man the earth becomes lovelier to one.' Wilde was contrasting his own treatment with the haunting memory of the half-witted lad who was flogged on doctor's orders in the jail.

Wilde's letter is one of the 'holy scriptures' of the English language, interpreting his saying that 'We are all in the gutter but some of us are looking at the stars.' How right that St Matthew's Gospel, drawing on Hosea, told the symbolic story of Joseph and Mary and Jesus fleeing to Egypt from the promised land. Christmas can be lived in exile even from the warmth of family and friends.

Those who serve churches receive many messages 'out of the deep', especially at Christmas and the new year. As John Donne pithily put it: 'More than kisses can, letters mingle souls.' No doubt in our IT days written letters will be fewer. Future W. H. Audens will not confidently write about the Night Mail with its 'Letters of thanks, letters from banks, letters of joy from girl and boy . . . And timid lovers' declarations and gossip, gossip from all the nations.'

When things were rough for Diana, Princess of Wales, she wrote:

Much has happened since we walked round St Paul's [before her wedding]. The most important thing I have learnt is the strength which comes from sharing what happiness I can with those you call 'on the margins'. I simply want to do it better. Incidentally, I am sure that Julian of Norwich is right.

It was Julian, writing the first book in English by a woman, who said 'All shall be well' – her experience was forged in deep psychological suffering.

In brief dark January days some may argue that Christmas gatherings and new year resolutions are best forgotten and that warmth and togetherness, trust and personal urgency must give way to the rule of market forces and the power struggle. But the relationship of love, not of exploitation, is at the heart of human life.

Rowan Williams has expressed the nature of charity, the love of which comes from God: 'Charity is a state in which bonds between people are treated as already established.' Faith sees this as a fundamental fact for which Christ was born and which lies at the heart of Christianity, the insight which saves us from anxious hesitations and guides us through the storm of events into a new year.

The Very Revd Alan Webster

Liberal Dean of Norwich and later of St Paul's who championed the ordination of women

Alan Brunskill Webster, priest: born Wrenbury, Cheshire 1 July 1918; ordained deacon 1942, priest 1943; Curate of Attercliffe Parishes, Sheffield 1942; Curate of St Paul's, Arbourthorne 1944; Chaplain and Vice-Principal, Westcott House 1946; Vicar of Barnard Castle 1953; Warden, Lincoln Theological College 1959–70; Canon and Prebendary, Lincoln Cathedral 1964–70; Dean of Norwich 1970–8; Dean of St Paul's 1978–87 (Emeritus); Hon. DD City University 1983; KCVO 1988; married 1951 Margaret Falconer (two sons, two daughters); died Cley next the Sea, Norfolk, 3 September 2007.

Alan Webster brought with him a new vision of a modernized cathedral when he became Dean of Norwich in 1970 and then Dean of St Paul's eight years later. At that stage, an appeal for a large sum to restore the historic fabric did not seem urgent. What seemed to be vitally needed was a change in the atmosphere. The great church must appeal to the public as a community with open doors, not as a museum or as a private club for the superior.

In Norwich, the Church of England's new form of Holy Communion, then an experiment, was introduced, with an altar in the centre of the congregation. Many less solemn meetings meant that the choices of the laity were heard and taken seriously. At other meetings, topics then in the news were expounded by experts and freely discussed.

Visitors were invited not only into the famous architecture, but also into a new shop and canteen, unprecedented lavatories and an exhibition which explained the Christian faith. Lawns and handsome houses owned by the cathedral covered 40 acres around it, but now this village was opened to the public by a riverside walk and houses were converted into a home for the elderly and a study centre with well-attended conferences and a library. It was said that 'The Close' became 'The Open'.

Webster took special pride in two enterprises: Cathedral Camps, which got young people working merrily on practical jobs in

Norwich and elsewhere; and a large hostel for men who would otherwise have slept rough.

The inspiration for this outreach was derived in particular by enthusiasm about a mystic in medieval Norwich, Mother Julian, the first woman to write a book in English and the first saint to insist that Christ's cross means not that God's wrath is satisfied by the punishment borne on behalf of sinners, but that God's love is proclaimed to be mother-like.

Many other cathedrals were stimulated to consider what could be learned and done in their own situations and the achievement was also noted in Downing Street. So in 1978, Webster was asked to apply his energy to the renewal of St Paul's Cathedral as a signal to London, to the nation and to the world. He accepted reluctantly.

As it turned out, he played a key role at several events. In 1981, the wedding between the Prince of Wales and Lady Diana Spencer delighted some 800 million television viewers as a magnificent affirmation of love and hope, and the cathedral did its best. And in the next year, the sombre service to mark the end of the Falklands war had undeniable integrity as an exhibition not of nationalism or of militarism but of a Christian response to a costly tragedy.

Webster's close friend Archbishop Robert Runcie preached a courageous sermon then and also commissioned a bold report on Britain's inner-city problems. In the extensive follow-up (including the Church Urban Fund), the message was taken to the powerful in the City of London by Webster. He risked alienating neighbours and benefactors, but instead the Lord Mayors chaired a committee of 'advisers' who advised not only the clergy but also their own colleagues, with the ultimate result that a massive sum was raised for the needs of St Paul's Cathedral after Webster's time.

Another campaign of great importance to the Church was the Movement for the Ordination of Women. Alan Webster's wife, Margaret, who had been very active in Norwich and who had wanted to be active in St Paul's, poured out her own energy as the movement's executive secretary (1979–86). In its slow triumph, her hard work, [wisdom and diplomacy] were vital.

But Alan's wife, and Alan himself, were not entirely happy in St Paul's. In Norwich, a conservative evangelical had been appointed as bishop when the liberal Websters were already installed, and now in London a bishop arrived who was to show where his heart lay by becoming a Roman Catholic. There were limits to what could be done when a diocese had such a leader.

In Norwich there had been some protests, at least in the early years, when the dean launched his projects without a full consultation with the residentiary canons who with him constituted the chapter, but in St Paul's tensions and disputes were far worse because the canons were more formidable. It was therefore with relief that in 1987 the Websters retired to Norfolk, first living amid a surviving circle of friends in Norwich and then enjoying a house by the sea. They were never idle.

Alan Webster wrote a book of memories and reflections entitled *Reaching for Reality* (2002). His other substantial book was a biography of a layman active in good works, Joshua Watson (1954). Alan Webster had seen the reality of a clergyman being the centre of life in a small village, because he was the only child of a person content to be that. When ordained himself, in 1943, after Shrewsbury School and Queen's College, Oxford, he saw how very little the Church could matter in a different environment, for he went as a curate and youth leader to wartime Sheffield, but he did a happy and creative spell as a parish priest in County Durham and threw himself into the training of outgoing priests, first in Westcott House, Cambridge, and then as Warden of Lincoln Theological College.

In Lincoln he had a Methodist on his staff, he invited a Roman Catholic to give regular lectures, he made sure that wives felt included, and he began to see what a cathedral must become.

David L. Edwards
Independent
5 September 2007

SOURCES AND ACKNOWLEDGEMENTS

The editors thank the following sources for permission to include the items here. All 'Credo' articles are from *The Times*. The source of the other published items is indicated.

Theme 1: Leaders and the Church

'Mikhail Gorbachev': Credo
'Robert Runcie': *Dictionary of National Biography* (*DNB*; extracts)
'Geoffrey Fisher': *DNB* (extracts)
'Leslie Hunter': *DNB* (extracts)
'David Sheppard' (extracts): *Guardian*
'Poul Hartling': *Church Times*
'Leslie Brown': *Independent*

Theme 2: World Peace, Justice and Tolerance

'Politicians as peacemakers': Credo
'Religion and honesty': Credo
'John Taylor': *Guardian*
'Prayer versus dogma': *The Times*
'Gonville ffrench-Beytagh': *Independent*
'A fusion of the spiritual and the secular': Credo
'Working together': Credo

Theme 3: Opening Up the Church

'Julian of Norwich': *Guardian*
'Florence Tim Oi Li' (by Alan and Margaret Webster): *Independent*
'Christian Howard': *Independent*
'Building bridges from the City': *Times*
'Constructive disagreement': Credo
'Can cathedrals share the sorrows and joys of their cities?': Credo
'The Church's one foundation': *Guardian*
'Alan Ecclestone': *Independent*
'Edward Carpenter': *Independent*

'Kenneth Sansbury': *Independent*
'Oliver Tomkins': *Independent*
'Horace Dammers': *Guardian*
'Jim Bishop': *Independent*
'Stanley Booth-Clibborn': *Independent*

Theme 4: The Church in Action

'Cure of Souls': SPCK (extract from *Reaching for Reality*)
'Launcelot Fleming': *Guardian*
'Kenneth Riches': *Independent*
'Edward Patey': *Guardian*
'Francis House': *Guardian*
'Frank Wright': *Independent*
'John Tinsley': *Independent*
'Joan Ramsey': *Independent*

Theme 5: Enriching Human Life

'All shall be well': Credo
'A stay in hospital is a lesson in the meaning and value of trust': Credo
'Rogues of profit still haunt the celestial road': Credo
'Three-fold core of religion, science and literature in the character of Sir
    Thomas Browne': *British Medical Journal*
'Petra Clarke': *Church Times*
'Tom Baker': *Independent*

Theme 6: Children and Young People

'God backs the poor': *The Times*
'Choice for changing faith': Credo
'Why the kids are all right': Credo
'High ideals for the next generation': Credo

Epilogue: Hope for the Future

'The journey towards understanding': Credo
'Everyday resurrections': Credo
'Love is at the heart of human life': Credo
'The Very Revd Alan Webster': *Independent*